A GALE OF CREATIVE DESTRUCTION

A GALE OF CREATIVE DESTRUCTION

THE COMING ECONOMIC BOOM 1992–2020

Myron H. Ross

FOREWORD BY LAWRENCE R. KLEIN
NOBEL LAUREATE

PRAEGER

New York
Westport, Connecticut
London

Library of Congress Cataloging-in-Publication Data

Ross, Myron H.
    A gale of creative destruction : the coming economic boom,
1992–2020 / Myron H. Ross.
        p.   cm.
    Bibliography: p.
    ISBN 0-275-93322-9 (alk. paper)
    1. Economic forecasting—United States.   2. United States—
Economic conditions—1981–   3. Long waves (Economics)—United
    States.   I. Title.
    HC106.8.R674   1989
    330.973—dc19   89-3556

Library of Congress Catalog Card Number: 89-3556
ISBN 0-275-93322-9

First published in 1989

Praeger Publishers, One Madison Avenue, New York, NY 10010
A division of Greenwood Press, Inc.

Printed in the United States of America

The paper used in this book complies with the
Permanent Paper Standard issued by the National
Information Standards Organization (Z39.48-1984).

10 9 8 7 6 5 4 3 2 1

Contents

Foreword

Myron Ross and I did not overlap at Pennsylvania, but we share many common economic views, almost as though we were educated together. We have a fondness for the older curriculum in which macroeconomics was taught in the course labeled "business cycles." I believe that a common thread in our thinking about macroeconomics—not to be confused with the contemporary (mis)treatment of that subject—is that overpowering influence of Simon Kuznets, his teacher and my respected colleague from the older (New York) tradition of the National Bureau of Economic Research. Simon taught our generation to look at economic history through the medium of statistical tables or charts. We learned that business cycles can be documented from a long historical record and that they call forth economic stories to explain their status as a separate phenomenon and specialized subject in economics.

When the stories are systematically put together with a carefully constructed statistical record, we find that the cyclical process is not just a chronology that can be mechanistically manipulated. That is why proponents of the view that the cycle has been eliminated will suffer the same fate as their predecessors and why uncareful historians who do not have the benefits of Simon's careful tutelage about statistics will repeatedly misread the trends, as distinct from the cycle, about the coming breakdown.

In the tradition of Simon Kuznets we have learned to appreciate the interactions of trend and cycle and also to appreciate the distinctions among short-run inventory movements, classical business cycles, and Kuznets' long swings. The long swings can be documented, but a problem remains in the case of long waves attributed to Kondratieff. They are very suggestive but not fully documented in the relatively brief sweep of quantitative economic history at our disposal.

We are inundated with sensational accounts of pending economic disaster, some of them reaching the bestseller lists. But these studies tend to be superficial, probably because their authors were not as advantaged as Myron Ross and I were through our association with Simon Kuznets and his Pennsylvania or National Bureau associates.

What I can fully appreciate in Myron Ross' account of economic history and its extrapolation into the next century is that it is well supported, in the Kuznets tradition, with quantitative backing. His stories fit well with the systematic collection of economic facts. While he may draw conclusions that are a shade more optimistic than mine, I do believe that we are going to avoid an economic Armageddon and that many of the reasons are those analyzed in the chapters of this book.

Myron Ross has not only a keen sense of history *cum* tools of economic analysis, but also a fine imagination. Reasons for being optimistic about our nation's and the world's economic future are not solely rooted in the past; they are, with a touch of imagination, contained in the present inventory of ideas, plans, or concepts from the fields of engineering and technology. Over the troubled and sluggish economic years of the 70s and 80s, we have been building up this inventory in biotechnology, telecommunications, materials science, microcircuitry, health care, and other fields.

Schumpeterian innovators have an ample store of new developments that await creative transfer from scientific discovery to commercial exploitation. Some of this exploitation has already occurred, only to lay the foundations for building on the shoulders of the first round of innovations, while others have not yet come to market but are destined to do so.

The coming economic era may not actually be a "boom," in Myron Ross' terms, but it is likely to be more expansionary than the difficult years after Vietnam, Watergate, the Oil Embargo, the Iranian Revolution, Black Monday, and a few other events of recent times.

Lawrence R. Klein

A GALE OF CREATIVE DESTRUCTION

1

Introduction

Certainly, in the movement of all these forces that weave the web of history, there is an obvious element of recurrence. Yet the shuttle which shoots backwards and forwards across the loom of Time in a perpetual to-and-fro is all this time bringing into existence a tapestry in which there is manifestly a developing design and not simply an endless repetition of the same pattern.[1]

No matter how refined and how elaborate the analysis, if it rests solely on the short view it will be ... a structure built on shifting sands.[2]

The United States is on the brink of a radical economic and social transformation. This will be a veritable revolution, though no Bastille will be stormed, nor will there be a Long March. The American economy, like other developed market-oriented economies, is subject to long waves or cycles, with periods of rising rates of economic growth over a period of a quarter of a century alternating with periods of declining rates of economic growth for another quarter of a century. In the early 1990s the United States economy will experience the beginning of a rising phase of a long wave, with the economy booming for two or three decades, interrupted only briefly by shallow recessions. Combined with some favorable structural changes in the economy, the fundamental underlying cause of the booming economy will be the momentum associated with a significantly above-average rate of technological advance. This "gale of creative destruction" will be associated with an unimagined increase in the level of living by the average American.

Because the United States will be on the rising phase of a long wave beginning in the 1990s, we can expect *per capita* real income to grow at an average annual rate of *at least* 2.5 percent.[3] If per capita income grows at an average rate of 2.5 percent annually, per capita income will double in 28 years for the average individual. Put differently, today's children can expect that when they are adults they will have *at least* twice the current income of their parents— a remarkable achievement.

A 2.5 percent minimum annual growth rate of per capita income is on the high side when compared with the past. Between 1839 and 1959, per capita income grew by 1.64 percent annually in the United States.[4] From 1950 to 1986, the annual per capita income growth rate was 2 percent. We can find per capita income growth rates higher than 2 percent if we arbitrarily select our beginning and ending years. For example, from 1938 to 1969 the annual per capita income growth rate was 2.6 percent; and from 1960 to 1969 it was 3.2 percent. Both 1938 and 1960 were years of depressed economic activity, so that the lower base year to start with increased the growth rate of income.

With these historical growth rates in mind, and with future favorable factors expected to occur (to be discussed in future chapters), it is not unreasonable to forecast a *minimum* average 2.5 percent growth rate of per capita income over the next couple of decades. In fact, it would not be surprising to see growth rates of per capita income averaging in the neighborhood of 3 percent.

In dealing with a relatively long period of 20 to 30 years, small differences in growth rates are highly significant. Gross national product (GNP) per capita in the United States in 1987 was $18,406. If real GNP per capita grows at 2 percent for 25 years, GNP per capita will grow to $30,435. If GNP per capita were to grow at 3 percent for 25 years, GNP per capita would be $38,965—a 28 percent higher GNP per capita level than with a 2 percent growth rate! Compounding has an almost magical quality.

Growth of income gives us control over the environment and increases our freedom. But growth of income is only one of the goals we seek to achieve. In addition to growth we would like to minimize both the unemployment rate and the degree of inequality. Further, we desire to minimize variations in income and the price level. And we seek to live in a world where there is international stability, where people, goods, and ideas are free to move between nations. All of these goals are to be pursued in the context of a democratic government with the market being the prime institution for allocating resources.

In the short run these goals are often in conflict so that we are faced with difficult trade-offs. However, in the long run—the orientation here—these goals tend to be complements of one another, for example, a higher rate of growth will reduce unemployment. Thus, if we achieve higher growth rates of income, it is likely that we will move toward achieving our other goals.

It should be noted that we are measuring economic development by GNP. However, GNP is a rough measure of development because it omits nonmonetary activity such as leisure and homework as well as other factors that come under the rubric of the "quality of life." An alternative measure of development to GNP is the physical quality of life index (PQLI) developed by the Overseas Development Council. The PQLI index is based on three indicators: the percentage of literacy, infant mortality, and life expectancy of those who are at least one year old. In the mid–1980s the index averaged 69, with Iceland, Norway, Sweden, Japan, and the United States all having an index of at least 97. Gambia and Somalia have an index of 16 to 17, respectively. The PQLI index is strongly correlated with per capita GNP. It is very difficult to conceive of a nation having a high level of economic development, as measured by the PQLI, without having a high level of GNP. The reverse is not necessarily true; for example, Kuwait has one of the highest GNPs per capita in the world, but has a PQLI of only 78.

Another approach to measuring welfare is taken by two Yale economists, William D. Nordhaus and James Tobin.[5] They amend net national product to include adjustments for such factors as the value of homework, leisure, and the negative urban externalities of pollution, noise, and litter. Nordhaus and Tobin find that between 1929 and 1965 their Measure of Economic Welfare increased at a significantly lower rate than did per capita GNP.

Even achieving all the economic goals discussed above would not necessarily lead to a good society. A higher level of GNP per capita may involve a lower ethical standard which permits us to indulge in our worst instincts. Economic growth makes civilization possible, but it is not inevitable.

Central to the thesis of this book is the existence of long cycles or waves. The idea of long cycles is very old. Among noneconomists it can be traced back to the Babylonians, the Greeks (particularly Plato and Pythagoras), the Romas, Vico, Machiavelli, and Nietzsche. In the twentieth century, we find the idea of long cycles articulated by Arthur Schlesinger[6] in applying cycle theory to political developments and Toynbee applying it to explain such broad historical developments as war and peace.

Turning to the thought of economists, the idea of long cycles first appeared in Hyde Clark's *Physical Economy* in 1847. Clark not only promulgated the idea of a 10-year cycle, but also believed that there were long cycles of 54 years duration. The idea of long cycles was also developed by the Dutch Marxist Van Gelderen in 1913. At about the same time, Pareto called attention to the tendency for prices, interest rates, and trade data to have a cycle of about one-half century's duration.

N. D. Kondratieff, who headed the Institute of Economic Research in Moscow, and Professor Joseph Schumpeter of Harvard did more systematic work on the long cycle and propagated the idea among economists. Both Kondratieff and Schumpeter argued that there is considerable empirical support for the long cycle or long wave taking place over a period of about 50 years. Furthermore, both economists (particularly Schumpeter) emphasized that at the heart of the long cycle was the development and diffusion of major innovations such as the steam engine, the building of railroads, electricity, and the automobile. Schumpeter underscored the point that innovations in technology tend to cluster in time, acting as a major cause of the long cycle, with emphasis being on the *disequilibrium* of economic forces. The ideas of Kondratieff and Schumpeter, particularly the latter, are fundamental in supporting the forecast that the next couple of decades will be a period of sustained prosperity and "good times."

Though the ideas of Kondratieff and Schumpeter on long waves are robust, with strong theoretical and empirical support (as we shall see in future chapters), these ideas have suffered great neglect. There are a number of reasons for this:

1. Probably the most important reason for this neglect is associated with the development of an alternative theory of long-run growth. The mainstream of current macroeconomic theory of the long run by academic economists is the neoclassical model of

growth. In many ways the neoclassical concept of growth is a superb intellectual achievement, in spite of its shortcomings. As developed by Professor Solow, in the neoclassical world there is a long-run dynamic full employment *equilibrium*—an equilibrium character-ized by an equality between planned savings and planned invest-ment, with the capital stock and income growing at the same *constant rate*. Empirical work, following in the spirit of the neo-classical model, indicates that as much as 40 to 90 percent of the growth of per capita income is caused by technological change. However, this powerful source of economic growth, technological change, is left in limbo. Technological change is assumed to take place at a *constant rate*, being exogenous, that is, technological change (like the weather) is a given, which causes changes in the economy, but which is not changed by it. Perhaps the reason for the assumption that technological change is exogenous and grows at the constant rate resides in the fact that technological change is difficult and unfamiliar to economists and often resists quantifi-cation.[7] But the assumption of a constant rate of technological change is only an assumption; and, if the assumption is in error (as will be shown in later chapters), the conclusions will likely be in error. Since classroom time is a scarce resource at the university, the neoclassical ideas tend to "crowd out" the ideas associated with Kondratieff and Schumpeter. Furthermore, the neoclassical ideas are often antithetical to theirs.

Most academic economists over the age of 50 can testify to the "crowding out" problem. In the 1950s it was common to have taught a course called Business Cycles in which much classroom time was devoted to discussing Schumpeter's ideas. By the 1960s their course was eliminated in many schools and a course called Income Analysis or Macroeconomics was put in its place. Following the fashion of the day, economists now concentrated on the neo-classical as well as Keynesian growth models, largely excluding discussion of Schumpeter's ideas. Economists can probably look back on these changes with considerable regret. Some balance should be brought back into macroeconomics by discussing the Keynesian and neoclassical ideas *and* the ideas of Schumpeter.

2. Kondratieff and Schumpeter's ideas were produced at a most inauspicious time. Kondratieff wrote his "The Long Waves in Eco-nomic Life" for a German periodical in 1926. However, it was not published in English until a decade later in the *Review of Economic*

Statistics in November 1935.[8] Schumpeter's *Business Cycles* appeared in 1939. In the 1930s the overriding problem was how to reduce large-scale unemployment, which was viewed as a short-run policy. The long run was of little interest.

3. Economists found it difficult to digest three great classics that appeared more or less simultaneously. Schumpeter's 1939 publication of *Business Cycles* had to compete with Leontief's classic analysis of input-output economics in 1936 ("Quantitative Input-Output Relations in the Economic System of the United States," *Review of Economics and Statistics*, August 1936), and Keynes's publication in 1936 of the *General Theory of Employment, Interest, and Money*. Keynes won the day, resulting in a significantly diminished attention to competing ideas.

4. Though long-run economic policy is important for the social and economic health of the nation, politicians usually ignore the long run because they concentrate on the short-run problem of getting reelected. The politicians' lack of a telescopic faculty exists because their constituents also place inordinate weight on the short run. The reason for this is clear. The long-run 50- to 60-year cycle is generally equal to or longer than the adult's life span, so that the long wave readily escapes the notice of individuals.

5. Schumpeter's *Business Cycles* is a poorly written book. Data are poorly organized and presented.

It is time to shift intellectual gears and to view long-run economic development in the spirit of Kondratieff and Schumpeter. This means that we will see economic development in the long run taking place cyclically, with technological change and population growth being endogenous. The probability of experiencing very good times with an annual average growth rate of per capita income of *at least* 2.5 percent should not be labeled "optimism" or Delphic mumblings. Rather, this conclusion or forecast can be supported by an examination of past history and a careful examination of the current economic scene. In a broad and general sense, the argument here is that history tends to repeat itself, as Toynbee suggested.

To maintain perspective, an outline of chapters that follow is provided:

Chapter 2: *Pessimistic Views*. In this chapter we will sample views that are pessimistic about the American economy. Frequently, these views will be in sharp contrast to the outlook developed here. This criticism of the critics will strengthen the underlying optimistic views developed in the remaining chapters.

Chapter 3: *Economic Long Waves in Retrospect*. There is persuasive evidence for concluding that economic history moves in long waves or long cycles, with a period of about 50 to 60 years duration. In particular, in examining the economic record since World War II in some detail, the argument will be developed that it is likely that the United States will experience the beginning of a rising long wave by the early 1990s.

Chapter 4: *The Accelerating Gale of Creative Destruction*. In this chapter the nature and causes of technological change will be examined. Stress will be placed on the fact that we can expect the rate of technological change to accelerate because of a concatenation of favorable economic forces. This will have a dramatic effect on increasing the growth rate of GNP per capita.

Chapter 5: *The Changing Structure of the Economy*. Technological change is not the only cause of change in the growth rate of per capita GNP. With the growth of the service sector relative to GNP, one can expect a more shallow short-run business cycle. By itself, this should contribute to a higher rate of growth of per capita GNP. Another very significant factor contributing to a higher growth rate of per capita GNP will be the diminished discrimination against minority and female workers. Not only will this increase the overall productivity per worker, but it will also diminish the degree of income inequality and the rate of poverty. Finally, one can expect unemployment rates to be below historical averages during the rising phase of the long wave.

Chapter 6: *The International Dimension*. Barriers to trade in goods, technology, and ideas have and will continue to come down. More and more, the world will look like a "one world" economy. On the production side, this is illustrated by the automobile with the American label. Though it has an American label, many of its parts have been produced in many different countries. The product is a world car—or perhaps we should say a "one world" car. Turning to the *consumption* side, we can expect per capita income for different nations to converge, with the consequence being that distribution of world income will become less unequal. As a result, there will be a convergence of tastes—tastes more or less akin to those associated with "Western" culture. These global patterns of consumer taste will complement the production side by increasing demand and permitting significant economies of scale in many industries. With parochialism dying throughout the world, there will be a significant stimulus to the growth of per capita GNP for the United States as well as the rest of the world. The great ascent of the next few decades will be a worldwide phenomenon.

Chapter 7: *The End of the Malthusian Specter*. The growth of *aggregate* income does not guarantee a growth of per capita income. A necessary, though not sufficient, condition for *per capita* income to grow is that population growth rates remain relatively low. It will be emphasized that rising economic growth rates tend to put a brake on population growth rates. The Malthusian specter that we will breed ourselves into poverty in the United States and the rest of the world is grossly exaggerated.

Chapter 8: *Government Policy*. Government policy can make a modest contribution to the goal of maintaining a sustained level of economic growth. Governments can stimulate economic growth by proper monetary and fiscal policy, by encouraging the growth of capital, and by maintaining a competitive market-oriented economy. At the very least, governments should do no harm.

Chapter 9: *Concluding Remarks*. Here we will weave all the strands from previous chapters into a coherent whole. Further, some of the noneconomic implications of the expected higher-than-average per capita growth rates will be examined. To repeat, a well-ordered economy makes civilization possible, and perhaps even more probable.

NOTES

1. Arnold Toynbee, *A Study of History* (Oxford University Press, Oxford, 1947), p. 235.

2. Jacob Viner, *The Long View and the Short* (Free Press, New York, 1958), pp. 112–13.

3. Throughout this book income will be in real terms, that is, nominal income will be adjusted for changes in the price level. Further rates of growth are in annual terms, with continuous compounding. Income equals GNP.

4. Raymond Goldsmith, testimony before the Joint Economic Committee, *Historical and Comparative Rates of Production, Productivity and Prices*, 86th Congress, 1st Session, 1959, part 2, p. 271.

5. William D. Nordhaus and James Tobin, *Is Growth Obsolete?* (National Bureau of Economic Research, Washington, D.C., 1972).

6. Arthur M. Schlesinger, Jr., *The Cycles of American History* (Houghton Mifflin, 1986). Also see George Modelski, *Long Cycles in World Politics* (University of Washington Press, 1987).

7. N. Kaldor and J. A. Mirrlees ("Growth Model with Induced Technical Progress," *Review of Economic Studies* 29, Oct. 1961) are exceptions among academic economists in that they argue that technological progress is induced by economic growth itself. But the model is noncyclical.

8. Kondratieff suffered an ignominious fate. Marxist economists generally rejected Kondratieff's idea that capitalism might gain renewed vigor. He ended as one of Stalin's victims, being exiled to Siberia.

2

Pessimistic Views

...capitalism inevitably and by virtue of the very logic of its civilization creates, educates, and subsidizes a vested interest in social unrest.[1]

As this book goes to press, pessimistic views of the future of the U.S. economy dominate. These conclusions diverge significantly from the optimistic tone of the views presented here. Of necessity, we have had to be selective in presenting these pessimistic views. The views presented here have been given a great deal of publicity during the last decade with most of the authors' books being best sellers. Discussion is confined to the United States—though one can find an array of similar foreign authors in other highly developed economies who view the future dimly.

Perhaps we can, following Schumpeter, dismiss these authors as "intellectuals." For Schumpeter, the "intellectual" is the nemesis of market-oriented capitalism. According to him, the intellectual has three attributes. First, intellectuals have the power of the spoken or written word. Second, intellectuals have no direct responsibility for everyday affairs. Finally, negative criticism will dominate the intellectuals' opinions in order to maintain their status as critics.[2]

The force of the intellectual's negative criticism is not constant. Intellectuals were held in abeyance during the relatively prosperous period from 1945 to the 1960s. During this period, per capita GNP rose by more than 2 percent annually and criticism was muted. But,

with the slowdown starting in the 1970s, there has been a prolif-
eration of negative criticism of the American economy. Perhaps we
can expect the likely prosperity beginning in the early 1990s to
again lower the level of negative criticism of the American economy.[3]

In any event, let us avoid invoking the argumentum ad hominem
and examine the arguments of our five authors on their merit.

PAUL KENNEDY, *THE RISE AND FALL OF GREAT POWERS*[4]

The historian Paul Kennedy, in a wide-ranging historical analysis
from 1500 to the present, attempts to explain why some nations
gain preeminence and then decline. His analysis focuses mainly on
Europe and the United States. In the last chapter (Chapter 7) he
moves away from historical analysis and predicts the relative decline
of America as an economic and world power. His argument is based
on two related contentions:

First, economic change is not uniform for different nations. Further, the U.S. economy will lag behind that of the rest of the world.

The argument in this book has been that there exists a dynamic for change,
driven chiefly by economic and technological developments, which then impact upon social structures, political systems, military power, and the position of individual states and empires. The speed of the global economic
change has not been a uniform one, simply because the pace of technological
innovation and economic growth is itself irregular . . . [5]

Second, this relative decline in American economic power will
imply a decline in the military power of the United States. With
slower growth, military expenditures will become a greater burden
for the United States. In Kennedy's words:

. . . this uneven pace of economic growth has had crucial long-term impacts
upon the relative military power and strategical position of the members
of the states system . . . the fact remains that all the major shifts in the
world's *military-power* balances have followed alterations in the *productive*
balances; and further, that the rising and falling of various empires and
states in the international system have been confirmed by the outcomes of
the major Great Power wars. . . . Victory has always gone to the side of the
greatest national resources.[6]

In a nutshell, the position of the United States as an economic and military power will diminish relative to the rest of the world in the next few decades.

The first argument is flawed empirically. It is true that Japan, China, Taiwan, South Korea, and Singapore have experienced a higher growth rate of income than the United States during the past decade. However, these higher growth rates are largely the result of starting from relatively low levels of per capita income. Baumol demonstrated[7] that there is a long-run tendency for income growth rates as well as per capita income levels to converge among industrialized nations. Once these low-income countries achieve a per capita income near that of other industrialized countries, their growth rates will converge to the level of the industrialized countries. Furthermore, during the past decade the U.S. income growth rates have exceeded those of Western and Eastern Europe, as well as the Soviet Union.

At another point Kennedy argues that the decline in American productive potential is evident by showing that the U.S. output as a percentage of world output in 1953 was 45 percent; by the 1980s this had been cut to about 22 percent. However, it is ridiculous to use 1953 as a base year, when European and Japanese economies were just recovering from the devastation of World War II. If we use a base year of 1938 or 1965, the United States's share of world output remains constant at about 22 percent. Put differently, this indicates that the U.S. growth rates of income since 1938 have been around the average of the growth rate for world output. There is no reason to believe that for the next few decades the United States' share of world output will be very different. To say that the United States economy will grow at a slower rate than China or other low-income countries appears to be accurate. But considering the low per capita income of China, this is a trivial conclusion. It is unlikely that Japanese growth rates of the last few decades can be sustained.

The second argument's main thrust is that the defense burden of the United States will increase. Kennedy believes that defense expenditures will crowd out investment, thereby limiting economic growth. Defense expenditures may also crowd out consumption. Thus, in spite of these defense expenditures, the slower economic growth will diminish the power of the United States in international affairs.

Like the first, the second argument is seriously flawed empirically.

Kennedy sees the size of the U.S. government deficit as a sign of the American loss of power. Yet he fails to make the same assertion with regard to the Japanese, who have an even higher deficit relative to GNP. Furthermore, the deficit of the federal government has been reduced since 1986. The deficit of the *federal* government in 1987 was 3.8 percent of GNP; the deficit of *all* governments, state and local as well as federal, was 2.6 percent of GNP in 1987. The magnitude of these deficits appears to be manageable if we experience relatively high rates of economic growth combined with modest expenditure reductions.

Another example of the misuse of data is Kennedy's assertion that the United States is a debtor nation. This is doubtful, since income received by Americans from foreign investments exceeded payments of income by Americans to foreigners on investments in the United States up to 1987. The data on foreign assets held by Americans abroad, as well as the data on U.S. assets held by foreign nations, is deficient. The data show book values, not market values. A large share of American investments took place in the 1950s and 1960s. Because of inflation their book value is far below their market value. Investments by foreigners in the United States are more recent, so that the difference between book value and market value is relatively small.[8]

Kennedy exaggerates the defense burden in the United States. Federal outlays for defense as a percentage of GNP have fallen from 9 percent in the 1960 to 1970 decade to about 6 percent in the 1976 to 1986 decade. Surely this decline should lead Kennedy to conclude that American economic power will be enhanced. But Kennedy is silent. In fact, Kennedy defines excessive defense expenditures (confined to a footnote on page 609) as expenditures on defense of 10 percent or more of GNP. By Kennedy's logic he should conclude that American defense expenditures are not excessive. But again Kennedy is silent. Rhetoric crowds out logic.

Kennedy confuses nominal and real values. On page 521 he speaks of a tripling of the American defense budget since 1970 and says this produced an increase of only 5 percent in the size of the armed forces on duty. The defense budget should be adjusted for changes in the price level since the size of the armed forces is a real variable. Again, he commits the same error when he says:

...the fact that the Reagan administration in the first term spent over 75 percent more on new aircraft than the Carter regime but acquired only 9 percent more planes points to the appalling military-procurement problems.[9]

Nominal expenditures should not be compared with real changes in the number of planes. He cites (as on page 442) a nominal increase in the price of particular weapons systems, but fails to adjust for changes in the price level and in the quality of the weapons systems.

All in all, *The Rise and Fall of Great Powers* suffers from the fallacy of emphasis, using and abusing selective statistics to support its conclusion. Exaggerating the magnitude of deficits or defense expenditures will not do. In addition, Kennedy exaggerates the power of the United States immediately after World War II. In these "good old days" a Communist revolution took place 150 miles off the coast of the United States. And America fought two bloody wars in Korea and Viet Nam. By comparison, the more recent picture is not as dismal as Kennedy portrays. There has been a trend toward democratization in many countries such as South Korea and the Philippines, consonant with U.S. policy. And the United States has been at peace since the early 1970s, while the Soviet Union had been bogged down in Afghanistan until 1989. While there have been failures of American foreign policy, it does not appear that there has been or will be serious military overextension or "imperial overreach." Finally, recognition of the importance of market forces in allocating resources by many Communist countries hardly speaks of a U.S. decline. Kennedy gives insufficient attention to the fact that the United States is a continental nation with a large resource base. The decline of other nations such as England and Spain involved nations with small resource bases and a colonial empire. The loss of empire meant the loss of power to these nations.

Empirical evidence aside, Kennedy fails to give sufficient attention to the ideological aspect. Military power alone is not sufficient to sustain an empire. Cultural preconceptions are an important cause for the imperial power to be accepted as superior by foreigners. The glory that was Athens came in the post-imperial period. Although Athens lost the war to Sparta—a war that lasted for nearly 30 years—she proceeded to conquer the world commercially as well as culturally. Sparta was ruined by its military success.

Finally, Kennedy fails to see the cyclical character in history. In dealing with empires and major nations, perhaps it is best to speak of phases of history or perhaps waves of history. We agree with Charles Wolfe's assessment of the book that,

... the rhetoric of decline is wrong, because it portrays a past that wasn't, a present that isn't and a future that probably won't be.[10]

MANCUR OLSON, *THE RISE AND DECLINE OF NATIONS*[11]

Mancur Olson believes that the U.S. economy will experience stagnation relative to other countries because of the emergence of powerful vested interests. Stable societies such as the United States, with a minimum of political and economic turbulence, evolve so that collusive organizations are generated. Other societies, such as Germany, Japan, and France, with their histories punctuated by the destruction of war, dictatorship, and political turbulence, have not had sufficient time to allow vested interests to become deeply rooted. Therefore, these nations have experienced and will continue to experience renewal and higher rates of growth than the United States.

The prime function of these collusive organizations is to redistribute income in their favor. In the process, economic efficiency is reduced. These collusive organizations tend to be conservative and to reduce the flexibility of the economy. Decision making is slower than it would be if there were individuals or firms making decisions. The net result is a reduction in the rate of economic growth.

There is no doubt that the collusive organizations can injure the economic fabric of the nation. The dire consequences of vested interests are evident in the United States. Few economists in the United States would support the current policy of massive farm subsidies or support the policy of restricting imports of steel, automobiles, and textiles. Unfortunately, Olson's thesis is not robust and much doubt is cast on the thesis from an empirical view.

1. Olson's book was published in 1982. He predicted that the United States and the United Kingdom—"stable" or "mature" societies—would have lower growth rates than France, West Germany, Italy, and Japan. Between 1983 and 1987, the two "mature" economies of the United States and the United Kingdom experienced average annual growth rates in GNP of 3.84 and 3.08 percent, respectively. In contrast, for the same period the "new" economies of France, West Germany, Italy, and Japan experienced average

annual growth rates in real GNP of 1.5, 2.28, 2.42, and 3.82 percent, respectively.[12] Note that the U.S. growth rate exceeded that of Japan as well as France, West Germany, and Italy. One would expect that the high Japanese growth rates of the past, which were export-led, cannot continue. As the Japanese balance of trade is reduced, growth rates will be reduced. Of course, it is recognized that in discussing national economic growth a five-year period is hardly definitive. Still, the data are inconsistent with Olson's thesis.

2. Olson probably exaggerates the power of vested interests. For one thing, the different vested interests are in competition with one another, so that there is some automatic tendency to limit some of the most pernicious consequences of vested interests. In fact, certain recent events appear to contradict Olson's thesis.

a. In 1986 in the United States, tax reform lowered marginal income tax rates and closed many loopholes, such as the investment tax credit. Why were the vested interests so weak in protecting their turf?

b. Since the late 1970s there has been a movement toward deregulation of many industries, such as banking, transportation, and telephones. Most of the established firms in these industries (as well as the unions) were against deregulation. Yet it occurred.

c. Standard practice has been for the U.S. Congress to approve new water projects—especially in an election year. Typically, new projects are funded at low levels in order to maximize the number of projects accepted and to satisfy the greatest number of members of Congress. But to most observers' amazement, in 1988 nine new flood control projects were rejected.[13]

3. Olson has difficulty in explaining the experience of Switzerland and Sweden. These two countries are considered stable and yet they have a good record of economic performance. At this point Olson resorts to ad hoc explanations. He argues that Switzerland's political structure constrains powerful lobbying organizations because it is extremely difficult to pass new legislation. However, this could be done in the United States with some moderate changes such as the requirement that all appropriation bills must have a two-thirds majority and/or that the president is given a line-item veto.

Sweden's good economic performance is explained by Olson by the presence and development of large encompassing special-interest organizations which have the incentive to take the general interest into account. Why does Sweden produce large encompassing special-interest organizations complementing Swedish economic growth, while the United States produces narrow special-interest organizations to the detriment of the American economy? Clearly Olson has difficulty in developing his ideas into a general theory. Exceptions hardly prove the rule, especially if there are too many exceptions.

4. Olson recognizes the power of international trade to limit the power of vested interests. However, he puts insufficient emphasis on this point. In fact, the success of the Swiss and Swedish economies is directly related to the fact that they are open economies, where domestic special-interest groups are usually powerless to control events beyond the boundaries of the local economy. Olson speaks approvingly that (quoting Thomas Jefferson): " . . . the tree of liberty must be refreshed from time to time with the blood of patriots and tyrants." Yet he fails to recognize the permanent revolution of technological change, particularly in an international context. If the rate of technological change is rapid—and this is our expectation for the future—there will be less opportunity for vested interests to become deeply rooted. The permanent revolution of technological change has the advantage over other revolutions in that it is bloodless.

5. In examining data in the United States, Olson believes the younger states, with fewer and weaker vested interests, will have a higher growth rate than the older states. In fact, he finds that there is a negative relationship between the growth of income of a state and the years since statehood was established. This, however, fails to deny the equally reasonable hypothesis that this negative relationship reflects a "catch up" problem for the new states with lower per capita income. While Olson recognizes this problem of observational equivalence, he does not resolve it. Put differently, the negative relationship may reflect a weak constellation of vested interests in the newer states *or* it may reflect the lower level of per capita income of the newer states which give it room for higher growth rates to catch up with those of the older states. Until the data can discriminate between the two hypotheses, the statistical results are of little value.

To summarize: Olson's arguments are not convincing empirically. He fails to recognize the power of competition among vested interests to constrain the negative consequences of vested-interest behavior. Nor does he recognize the power of such ideas as deregulation and tax reform to constrain the behavior of vested interests in the longer run. Like Mark Twain's death, the stagnation of the American economy is exaggerated.

LESTER C. THUROW, *THE ZERO-SUM SOLUTION*[14]

Lester Thurow believes that the U.S economy is on a perilous path if current policies remain unchanged. An American version of peristroika is required. He concludes that, if the United States does not adopt an industrial policy, GNP per capita will be half that of the leading industrial country in 50 years. America is going the way of Great Britain during the turn of the century if it does not choose to reform its policies.

The key to understanding Thurow's pessimistic outlook lies in his belief that in the long run productivity in the United States will lag behind that of other industrial nations. The productivity lag is the bete noir causing the problem of the balance-of-trade deficit and the deficit in the federal government's budget.

He objects to the solution of the trade deficit which would require significant reductions in the exchange rate. While he agrees that this would reduce the trade deficit, the consequences are all bad. Significant decreases in the value of the dollar would increase the price of imports and lower the American standard of living. To the extent that productivity is increased, the need for a decrease in the value of the dollar is diminished. In Thurow's words:

With low productivity growth there is no alternative. The dollar must and will fall. To hold exchange rates up is simply to drive American firms out of business. Their prices gradually become less and less competitive and they lose market share at home and abroad. If the dollar falls, the United States is competitive in a narrow sense that it has a balance in its balance of payments, but it becomes less and less competitive in terms of standard of living.[15]

Thurow holds that Reagan administration policies were misguided. Tax cuts unaccompanied by expenditure cuts have led to large deficits in the federal government's budget *and* the balance of trade. These deficits in the federal government's budget increased interest rates in the United States relative to the rest of the world, with the consequence that the demand for dollars increased and the value of the dollar increased rapidly. The high value of the dollar in turn caused large deficits in the U.S. balance of trade. Thus the two deficits are intimately linked.

Thurow suggests a variety of policies which would eliminate the current problems:

1. To improve productivity, the quality of the educational system must be improved. Among required changes would be to extend the school year from 180 to 240 days.

2. An industrial policy is required which would bring the government into a partnership with the private economy. Industrial policy is a vehicle for bringing about a strategic consensus between government, industry, and labor as to long-term goals. Since we will discuss industrial policies below, there is no need to repeat the discussion here.[16]

3. The federal government's budget should be brought into balance by a tax increase. Thurow believes that it is not possible to significantly cut expenditures. Defense expenditures cannot be reduced significantly because of the constraints of foreign policy. And transfer payments to the elderly cannot be reduced significantly because it would be a political hot potato. And, finally, interest cost cannot be cut since such payments are obligatory.

4. Thurow concludes that the American economy is becoming more and more unfair as measured by the distribution of income. As evidence for this, he shows that between 1969 and 1982 the income share going to the lowest half of the income distribution of all American families fell from 23 to 20 percent. "... to obtain the efficiency the United States needs, it is going to have to promote equity."[17]

There are many problems with Thurow's analysis. If his analysis were correct, his predictions should be correct. Unfortunately for Thurow, his short-term predictions are far off the mark, casting serious doubt on his analysis. Between 1985 and 1987, defense expenditures fell in real terms as well as a percentage of GNP. Furthermore, *net* transfer payments to the elderly have been reduced by taxing social security income beginning in 1986. And between 1985 and 1987 interest payments by the federal government have been reduced relative to the size of the budget or GNP.

The two deficits are falling. Between 1985 and 1987, the federal government budget deficit fell from $196.0 billion to $152.6 billion. And the trade deficit has been reduced since 1986.

It should be noted that the trade-weighted value of the dollar was at about the same level in 1987 as in 1977. The illusion that the dollar has fallen excessively results, in part, from the fact that the dollar started its decline from historically very high levels in the early 1980s. The media, in particular, have engaged in the fallacy of emphasis by citing the decline in the value of the dollar relative to the yen, as if this were the typical change in the value of the dollar with regard to all currencies.

Thurow overestimates the required decline in the value of the dollar for two reasons. First, he implies that price elasticities for internationally traded goods are low. This is true in the short run, but is false in the intermediate and long runs. How much the exchange rate is required to fall to eliminate the trade balance depends on elasticities. If the elasticities have a high absolute value, small reductions in the value of the dollar will be sufficient. For example, if the elasticity of demand with regard to price is -2.5, a 10 percent reduction in exchange rates will increase export volume by 25 percent, so that the dollar value of exports will increase by 15 percent.

Second, if the United States has a positive balance in capital movements, that is, more financial investment is made in the United States than Americans invest in foreign nations, an offsetting deficit in the trade balance is required. One should not confuse the trade balance, which deals with exports and imports of goods, with the balance of payments, which deals not only with exports and imports of goods but also with international financial transactions. Apparently the United States has been an attractive host to foreign financial investments because of its relatively stable economic and social conditions. For many foreigners, investment in the United States offers a good return with little risk. From this vantage point the deficit in the American trade balance is not a problem but is a symbol of the American success story.

Writing in 1985, Thurow said:

Americans were enjoying the thrill of a cyclical recovery in 1984, but ahead lie more sickening bouts with inflation and unemployment, for the nature of the system has not been altered.[18]

Again Thurow misses the boat. Unemployment rates were not stuck at 7.0 to 7.5 percent, but by 1989 had come down to 5.1 percent. And since 1985 the United States has experienced one of the highest growth rates of GNP of any industrialized nation.

But all the above relates to the short run. In the long run, Thurow's forecasts appear to be as bad as his short-term forecasts. First, his arithmetic underlying the assertion that per capita GNP will be half that of the leading industrial nation in 50 years is, to say the least, an exaggeration. Let us assume that the anonymous "leading industrial nation" and the United States have the same current GNP per capita. Also assume that the U.S. GNP per capita grows at a 2.0 percent annual rate over a period of 50 years—modest by historical standards. If the "leading industrial nation's" per capita GNP is to be double the per capita GNP of the United States, it would require a growth rate of 3.4 percent for the "leading industrial nation." A 3.4 percent increase over a 50-year period is unlikely.

The long-run forecast is questionable because it is based on an analysis of the short 1975 to 1985 period. In doing this, Thurow ignores Darby's long-run analysis of the productivity decline.[19] Darby believes that productivity will return to higher levels in the 1990s because of demographic changes in the labor force. Thurow's conclusion that there will be sizeable differences in national productivity levels over the long run have not been true in the past, as Baumol shows,[20] and will no doubt not be true in the future. We can expect most industrialized countries to enjoy higher productivity growth rates over the next few decades, but it is doubtful that international differences will be significant.

Finally, Thurow is perhaps too hard on American education. Scholastic aptitude test scores have improved over the past five years and teachers' real wages have increased. And foreign students "vote with their feet" by revealing a preference for American universities. They must be doing something right!

RAVI BATRA, *THE GREAT DEPRESSION OF 1990*[21]

Ravi Batra believes that

...all the evidence indicates that another great depression is now in the making, and unless we take immediate remedial action, the price we will have to pay is catastrophic.[22]

And, again:

I believe that a disaster of the same, if not greater, severity (than the Great Depression of the 1930s) is already in the making. It will occur in 1990 and plague the whole world through at least 1996.[23]

In contrast to the forecast of the present volume, Batra's thesis is quite pessimistic. Where the present volume predicts that the next 25 years will be, on average, quite prosperous, Batra's book forecasts 6 years of a Great Depression. Given the differences in the time horizon of these two forecasts, it is not logically impossible for these two conclusions to be true; that is, it is possible to have a depression for 6 years, followed by about 19 or 20 years of a super boom, However, the probability of both forecasts occurring is practically zero. We believe that if there are short cyclical declines in the economy they will be quite modest, contrary to Batra's prediction.

Batra concludes that the money supply and the price level have a regular cycle, reaching peaks every 30 years. The decade of the 1970s was the last peak, so that we can now expect the money supply to decline until about 1990, reaching a peak again in the year 2000.

Behind the variation in the money supply is the variation in the distribution of wealth. As this distribution becomes more unequal, a speculative mania results, eventually provoking a banking crisis. The wealthy segment of the population become less risk-averse and take on riskier investments. Those in the middle and poorer end of the distribution have less collateral and thereby become less creditworthy. Thus the increasing concentration of wealth increases the number of banks with relatively risky loans, increasing the probability of banks going bankrupt. The stage is now set for a financial crisis.

To avoid the impasse of a great depression, Batra suggests certain policies for the short term. Among these policies are: a federal property tax should be imposed on the wealthiest 1 percent of the population; the government should prohibit banks from lending money for corporate takeovers; and higher margin requirements should be imposed on commodity traders. More fundamental reforms would involve a redistribution of wealth. For example, a ceiling would be placed on wages, with the maximum wage being no higher than 10 times the minimum wage; and there should be a ceiling placed on inherited wealth.

An assessment of Batra's book is difficult because of the crucial role of the distribution of wealth. First, the distribution of wealth data for the top 1 percent is hardly a proxy for the entire distribution of wealth. Second, the distribution of wealth data varies with movements in common stock prices. When there is a bull market, the distribution of wealth becomes less equal, as in 1929 prior to the stock market crash and in 1987 prior to October 19. And when there is a bear market, the distribution of wealth becomes more equal as in 1933 and in 1987 after October 19. Third, the wealth data are incomplete. They do not include human capital. Fourth, Batra exaggerates the extent of inherited wealth. Most studies have shown that between 10 and 18 percent of wealth is inherited.[24]

Batra, in effect, has a stock market theory of the business cycle, since variations in stock market values are the basic causes for the variations in the distribution of wealth. There are at least two problems with such a theory. It is true that common stock prices appear to be a leading indicator of the short-term cycle—though this does not necessarily imply cause and effect. Unfortunately, variations in common stock values often give false signals. Between 1946 and 1986, 13 percent of the turns in the business cycle were not accompanied by a turn in the stock market. And 45 percent of the time, stock market turns were not accompanied by turns in the business cycle.[25] Not a very good forecasting record!

A second problem with a stock market theory of the business cycle is that a decline in stock market values is consistent with Schumpeter's view of the cycle. As a wave of innovation comes to an end after a period of gestation, profit rates will fall and result in a decline in stock market values. A stock market decline is also consistent with Milton Friedman's view that the prime cause of the business cycle is variation in the money supply. A sudden decrease in the money supply will initially raise interest rates, eventually curtailing spending and producing a recession. At the same time, stock market values will fall.

Batra says,

...the 1970s were unmistakably the most recent peak of the cycle. Money growth in the 1980s has declined, though not by much.[26]

In fact, from 1970 to 1979 the money supply, defined as M2, grew at a 9 percent annual rate. And between 1980 and 1987 the money supply grew again at an annual rate of 9 percent.[27] There is no peak in the 1970s. If the peak vanishes, does the Great Depression of 1990 vanish?

Finally, Batra is oblivious to structural changes in the economy since the Great Depression of the 1930s. The increased importance of government spending as a percentage of GNP will moderate the business cycle. Unemployment compensation will help limit the severity of a recession. In addition, as we shall indicate below, the growing importance of the service sector will diminish the importance of inventory variations and moderate the business cycle. And the presence of bank deposit insurance is probably a bulwark against a banking crisis occurring.

Batra's book is found wanting.

BEN WATTENBERG, *THE BIRTH DEARTH*[28]

We are reluctant to include Ben Wattenberg among the pessimists or naysayers because in other books Wattenberg is quite sanguine and optimistic about the American economy. Nevertheless, *The Birth Dearth* should be included since Wattenberg believes some fundamental demographic problems can be expected in the United States and other industrialized democracies.

The basic theme of *The Birth Dearth* is that the industrialized democracies are not producing enough babies. These industrialized democracies comprise 22 nations—the United States, Canada, all the Western European countries, Japan, Australia, New Zealand, Israel, and Iceland. The total fertility rate (i.e., birth rates for women of child-bearing ages) for all major industrialized countries has fallen below the replacement rate of 2.1.[29] Only Ireland, Israel, and New Zealand have total fertility rates exceeding 2.1. This signifies that population growth will decline for the United States as well as for the industrialized democracies by the decade 2020, roughly the end of the fifth Kondratieff "rise." Wattenberg also emphasizes the *relative* decline of population in the industrialized democracies. In 1985 the 22 industrialized democracies were 15 percent of total world population. It is projected that by 2030, the 22 industrialized democracies will be only 9 percent of total world population. Wattenberg does not believe that immigration will make much difference in the population growth rates.

The declining rate of population growth will present serious problems for the United States and other industrialized democracies. From an economic perspective, the birth dearth produces two interrelated problems: shrinking markets and an older population. In Wattenberg's words:

This (declining population growth rate) should provide plenty of food for thought for businessmen looking ahead; for young people who one day will be not-so-young, in businesses that face shrinking markets; for middle-aged people who will soon be older and wondering where their federal Social Security pension money will come from; for people who may one day sell a house and not find a buyer at a reasonable price. In short, it is food for thought for almost everyone.[30]

The outlook for the housing industry (including those who provide equipment and furniture for housing), a producer of roughly 10 percent of all employment in the United States, is bleak:

People typically buy their first house when they are young. That makes sense; that's when they (typically) marry and (typically) have children, even if only one. In 1990, according to Census data, the number of young Americans aged 25 to 34 will be *44 million*. But by the year 2000 because of the onset of the Birth Dearth in the early 1970s the number of young people aged 25 to 34 will be only *36 million*. That is a one-decade *decline* of young adults of 18 percent—while the United States is still growing.... That's bad for the housing industry and people who work in the housing industry.[31]

Not only is the outlook for the housing industry bleak, but it is bleak for other industries as well because of shrinking markets caused by the birth dearth. Wattenberg believes that the birth dearth will cause problems in many industries. He holds that modern market-oriented economies rely heavily on expanding markets. As the phase of an expanding population comes to an end there will be economic turbulence. More and more firms, faced with shrinking markets, will find it increasingly difficult to maintain a satisfactory profit.

The cheerless view of population growth extends to the aging of the population. Wattenberg forecasts that the current dependency ratio will fall from five workers supporting one elderly person to two persons supporting one elderly person by 2030. If population growth rates are not reversed and nothing is done, the social security system will go broke by the middle of the next century. The time when the system goes broke may be delayed if old-age benefits are lowered, fewer Medicare benefits are provided, or if retirement is delayed. It should be noted that the social security system has moved in these directions. Some social security benefits became taxable, and the retirement age was extended to 67 by the year 2022 if one wishes to receive full benefits. In addition, hospital benefits have been constrained by setting prospective (rather than retrospective) prices on certain medical outputs.

The lower total fertility rate by the industrialized nations also results in three other problems. First, Wattenberg holds that there will be a decline in the quality of the population because lower-income families have a higher total fertility rate than families in the middle- and upper-income levels. Second, he believes that democratic "Western" values are endangered because of the relative decline of population in the industrialized democracies. Finally, he believes that, because of shrinking markets, the incentive to innovate will be lessened so that economic growth will be reduced. There will be no rising tide of technological change.

Can nothing be done? Wattenberg does not accept these conclusions as inevitable. He recommends many different policies to stimulate the output of babies. On his "grocery list" of policies are: cash payments to families having babies, extensive use of day care facilities by firms, reduced taxes for larger families, flexible work time, and maternal leave for women.

Wattenberg's book deflates the proposition that overpopulation in the industrialized countries is a problem. But his thesis that these countries will suffer from underpopulation has its problems.

1. Wattenberg equates population size with the size of markets. Effective demand for goods requires income. Individuals without income have no impact on effective demand—though they may have needs or desires. If per capita income grows over the next 25 years at a rate of 2.5 to 3.0 percent as argued here, demand will grow at an increasing rate even though population growth rates will be falling. For example, aggregate demand for goods by Americans is significantly higher than the Chinese aggregate demand even though China has five times the population of the United States.

Wattenberg believes that the total fertility rate of the low-income nonindustrialized nations is too high. In his terms, these low-income nations should provide an enormous source of demand for the output of the industrialized nations. But he rejects this as a solution to the industrialized nations' problems. He now recognizes the link between income and demand—a link he ignored in most of the book. He asks:

Where will the dollars, francs, guilders, lire, deutschemarks and pounds come from to buy European goods, if Europeans, due to low population, can't buy very much, thereby sending those hard currencies overseas?[32]

The answer to this question is that high income growth rates of the industrialized nations will generate imports from the nonindustrialized nations. The increased exports of the nonindustrialized nations in turn will generate a demand for imports from the industrialized nations. Export supply creates import demand. Say's law is alive and well!

2. Another stricture refers to Wattenberg's outlook with regard to housing. Demand for housing, like other goods, depends on income. Thus we cannot be sure that housing demand will fall. In fact, there may be an increase in demand for better quality housing with the higher per capita income growth rate expected.

Furthermore, even if the demand for housing declined, the demand for other goods would increase. For example, as the population ages, the demand for travel probably becomes more important and the derived demand for automobiles increases. Thus, automobile demand offsets housing demand to some degree. If housing demand declines, the housing component of national income will also decline. Because housing has great durability relative to other goods, it is a major factor determining the amplitude of the short-term business cycle. This should improve economic performance.

3. Wattenberg underestimates the qualitative improvement in the population as a growth rate of population falls. For one thing, an older and more experienced labor force is usually more productive than a younger, less experienced one. Furthermore, as the number of children decline in a family, one would expect that the quality of the children would increase—at least from an economic point of view. For example, one child from a middle-income family may, as an adult, become an engineer earning $60,000, while a child from a lower-income family may earn $20,000 as a factory worker. In economic terms, the two children are not to be equated. Finally,

many of the industrialized nations are selective about the quality of immigrants, thereby enjoying the fruits of the "brain drain"—to the detriment of the nonindustrialized nations. For example, a doctor migrating from India to the United States is a great boon to the American economy.

Not only does Wattenberg underestimate immigrants qualitatively, he also underestimates them quantitatively. In 1987, 601,516 *legal* immigrants entered the United States—probably more immigrants than all other countries in the world accepted. This was about 28 percent of the increase in the U.S. population in 1987. Finally, it should be noted that, even if immigrants are of average quality from an economic point of view, they are still a "bargain" from the vantage point of the United States. Adults tend to dominate among the immigrants, so that no school expenditures or other expenditures for children are required.

While immigrants are a "bargain" in the long run, they tend to reduce the U.S. growth rate of per capita income in the short run. This happens because initially the income of immigrants usually falls below the U.S. average, so that the growth of aggregate income will lag behind the growth of population. However, after about a decade the income of immigrants exceeds the income of native-born Americans and growth rates will be enhanced.

4. Wattenberg exaggerates the difficulties expected for the social security system in the twenty-first century. Given the great difficulties in population forecasting, one would expect experts to disagree. Munnell disagrees with Wattenberg's contention that the total fertility rate will be between 1.6 and 1.8 when she says:

... the social security intermediate projection of a long-run fertility rate of 2.0 appears more likely than either the optimistic or pessimistic projections of 2.3 or 1.6, respectively. That is, it would be very difficult to make a convincing case for a fertility rate assumption substantially different from that incorporated in the Trustees' intermediate projections.[33]

Furthermore, modest tax rate increases may prevent the system from going broke.

To even discuss the outlook for social security after the year 2057 verges on the ridiculous.... Nevertheless, for the sake of completeness, it is probably useful to mention ... that the reserves that are scheduled to accumulate during the period 1990–2020 will be exhausted by 2057. Hence the OASDI payroll tax rate will have to be raised under the intermediate assumptions by roughly 1 percentage point each for employees and employers in the middle of the next century to cover the costs of the program.[34]

If there is average economic growth in per capita income of 2.5 to 3.0 percent, nominal wages will grow faster than the price level, that is, real wages will grow. This means that social security tax receipts (dependent on nominal wages) will grow faster than social security index benefits (dependent on the price level). The social security system appears to be in good health. The graying of the American population is manageable economically as well as politically.

In summary, Wattenberg's *The Birth Dearth* has its problems. Aggregate demand is confused with the size of population, and the impact of housing on the state of the economy is exaggerated. Innovation does not depend on population size. Rather, it depends in part on the expected growth of income. And, given the accelerating pace of technological change and favorable structural changes expected, as discussed below, one can expect a high and rising growth rate in per capita income over the next 25 years or so. This will prevent the social security system from going broke.

Let us summarize the criticism of the critics. Except for Batra, the authors cited above fail to recognize the long-run cyclical nature of the economy. By assuming that the period of stagnation in the 1970s is a more or less permanent state, these authors are inevitably bound to forecast doom and gloom. This failure leads also to a failure to recognize the great technological opportunities that lie ahead. Finally, all the authors have inadequately buttressed their arguments empirically. Having cleared the decks of these pessimistic views, the door is open to a more optimistic view of the future developed in the remaining chapters.

NOTES

1. Joseph Schumpeter, *Capitalism, Socialism and Democracy* (Harper & Row, New York, 1947), p. 146.

2. Schumpeter, *Capitalism, Socialism and Democracy*, p. 147.

3. For an interesting view that the intellectual's impact is cyclical, see: James R. Schlesinger and Almarin Phillips, "The Ebb Tide of Capitalism? Schumpeter's Prophecy Re-examined," *Quarterly Journal of Economics* (August 1959).

4. Paul Kennedy, *The Rise and Fall of Great Powers* (Random House, New York, 1987).

5. Kennedy, *Rise and Fall*, p. 439.

6. Kennedy, *Rise and Fall*, p. 439.

7. See pp. 120–22.

8. There is nothing inherently wrong with being a debtor nation; or for that matter there is nothing inherently good about it. For an under-developed country, debtor status in the early stages of development is reasonable. Underdevelopment may be defined as a general situation where there are profitable investment opportunities from a social point of view. Given this definition, is the United States an underdeveloped country? Low per capita income is not a sufficient condition for being classified as under-developed nor does high income per capita necessarily exclude a country from being classified as underdeveloped.

9. Kennedy, *Rise and Fall*, p. 522.

10. Charles Wolf, "America's 'Decline': Illusion and Reality," *Wall Street Journal*, May 12, 1988, p. 22.

11. Mancur Olson, *The Rise and Decline of Nations* (Yale University Press, New Haven, CT, 1982).

12. *Economic Report of the President, 1988*, p. 374.

13. "Congress is Closing Tap on Spending for Water Projects," *Wall Street Journal*, May 12, 1988, p. 48.

14. Lester C. Thurow, *The Zero-Sum Solution* (Simon and Schuster, New York, 1985).

15. Thurow, *The Zero-Sum Solution*, p. 97. Note that Thurow here is con-fusing the balance of trade with the balance of payments. If the United States has a positive balance in capital movements, this would require a deficit in the U.S. trade balance to have an equilibrium in the balance of payments.

16. See pp. 256–59.

17. Thurow, *The Zero-Sum Solution*, p. 120.

18. Thurow, *The Zero-Sum Solution*, p. 31.

19. See p. 52.

20. See pp. 120–22.

21. Ravi Batra, *The Great Depression of 1990* (Simon and Schuster, New York, 1987).

22. Batra, *Great Depression*, p. 20.

23. Batra, *Great Depression*, p. 20.

24. Franco Modigliani, "The Role of Intergenerational Transfers and Life Cycle Savings in the Accumulation of Wealth," *Journal of Economic Perspectives* (Spring 1988), p. 19.

25. Victor Zarnowitz, "On Causes and Consequences of Financial In-stability," *Economic Outlook, USA* (Winter 1987/88), National Bureau of Economic Research, p. 14.

26. Batra, *Great Depression*, p. 83.

27. *Economic Report of the President, 1988*, p. 325.

28. Ben Wattenberg, *The Birth Dearth* (New York: Pharos Books, 1987).

29. Two parents must be replaced by two children. The extra 0.1 required is because of infant mortality, which adds 0.05 to the required rate and because more male babies are born than female babies, which adds another 0.05 to the required rate.

30. Wattenberg, *Birth Dearth*, p. 55.

31. Wattenberg, *Birth Dearth*, p. 57 (emphasis on original).

32. Wattenberg, *Birth Dearth*, p. 62.

33. Alicia Munnell, "The Outlook for Social Security in the Wake of the 1983 Amendments," in Myron H. Ross (ed.), *The Economics of Aging* (The W. E. Upjohn Institute for Employment Research, 1985), p. 33.

34. Munnell, "Outlook for Social Security," p. 34.

3

Economic Long Waves in Retrospect

...some processes covered by our concept of innovation must take a much longer time than others to have full effect. The railroadization or electrification of a country, for instance, may take between one-half and the whole of a century and involve fundamental transformations of its economic and cultural patterns, changing everything in the lives of its people up to their spiritual ambitions.[1]

There are long waves in the evolution of the economy of 48 to 60 years duration. These long waves, particularly the rising segment, are quiet revolutions restructuring the pattern of production and consumption. The term "long waves" is preferred to that of "long cycles," because the latter term often connotes a constant periodicity. However, it should be noted that the "long waves" are no less periodic than the shorter business cycles. On the existence of "long waves" and their periodicity, Kondratieff is clear:

The relevant data which we are able to quote covers about 140 years. The period comprises two and one-half cycles only. Although the period embraced by the data is sufficient to decide the existence of long waves, it is not enough to enable us to assert beyond doubt the cyclical character of these waves. Nevertheless we believe that the available data are sufficient to declare this cyclical character to be very probable.

It has been objected that long waves lack the regularity which business cycles display. But this is wrong. If one defines "regularity" as repetition in regular time intervals, then long waves possess this characteristic much as the intermediate ones. A strict periodicity in social and economic life does not exist at all—neither in the long nor the intermediate waves. The length of the latter fluctuates at least between 7 and 11 years, i.e., 57 percent. The length of the long cycles fluctuates between 48 to 60 years, i.e., 25 percent only.[2]

Kondratieff adds that there is simultaneity and similarity for different time series. And he demonstrates that the long waves are an international phenomenon, with fluctuations between European countries and the United States moving in parallel fashion.

It should be observed that current usage of the term "business cycle" most often refers to a cycle of three to five years duration. These short cycles, like the intermediate cycles of 7 to 11 years (referred to above by Kondratieff), fluctuate with a variable length of time at least exceeding 25 percent.

Kondratieff's method was straightforward. If there was a trend in an economic time series, as in output, he divided by population size. He then determined deviations from the trend. The data examined were from England, France, Germany, and the United States. He observed financial data such as interest rates and commodity prices, as well as production data on such products as coal and iron. All told, he examined 24 time series from 1790 to 1914–20.

In this chapter we shall examine the evidence for long waves. In doing this we shall try to complement Kondratieff's observations with a broad-brush view of American economic history. To make a reasonable forecast of the American economy for the next 25 years or so, it is important to understand and appreciate the past evolution of the American economy. The purpose is *not* to tell the fascinating story of the development of the American economy— though this is important. Rather, the main purpose is to focus on broad patterns of events which tend to have a repetitive quality. We do not want the trees (historical detail) to hide the forest (basic patterns of economic development). This view of American economic history offers persuasive evidence that the basic pattern of economic history in market-oriented economies involves surges of clustering of innovations interacting within the constraints of monetary and fiscal policy in an international setting. These surges of innovation are the basic underlying rhythm for the short-term and long-term economic cycle.

We are not falling into the trap of what Karl Popper called his-

Table 3.1
Long Waves in the U.S. Economy

Wave	Phase	Period[a]		Number of Years[b]	Real Per Capita Income	
					In 1958 Dollars[c]	Growth Rate
First Wave:	Rise	1790 to	1810–17	20	NA	NA
	Decline	1810–17 to	1844–51	34	NA	NA
Second Wave:	Rise	1844–51 to	1866	22	NA	NA
	Decline	1867 to	1890–96	23	$531[d]	--
Third Wave:	Rise	1890–96 to	1914–20	24	836	1.7
	Decline	1914–20 to	1938–45	24	1267	0.6
Fourth Wave:	Rise	1938–45 to	1969	31	1484	2.6
	Decline	1970 to	1992–94	22	3555	1.6[e]
Fifth Wave:[f]	Rise	1992–94 to	2017–2021	25	--	at least 2.5 likely 3.0

[a]The first three waves are from Kondratieff's dating, except the concluding date of the third wave (1938–45), which is the author's dating. The fourth and fifth (forecast) waves are also the author's dating.

[b]Calculated from the earliest year, e.g. for the 'rise' of the third wave we have 1914 minus 1890 or 24 years.

[c]To 1970 calculated from <u>Historical Statistics of the United States Colonial Times to 1970</u>, Series F 1–5, U.S. Department of Commerce, 1971. Per capita incomes are for the first year of each period, e.g. per capita income in 1914 is $1,267.

[d]No growth rate is calculated for 1867 to 1890–96 because per capita income of $531 is an average of 1869–1878. 1867 per capita income was probably higher than $531 in the earlier part of the period because per capita income probably declined significantly with the prolonged 1873 depression.

[e]Real GNP growth rate less the population growth rate was calculated from data in <u>Economic Report of the President, 1988</u>, pp. 259, 283. The fourth wave 'decline' was calculated to 1987.

[f]Forecast.

toricism. *Historicism* is defined as the propensity to pronounce "laws of history" and to derive from them forecasts that cannot be tested by the procedures of social science. However, Popper was clear that prediction is possible in the case of repetitive systems, of which long cycles are an example.

Table 3.1 depicts four long waves in American economic history from 1790 to 1992 and beyond. Each long wave is broken down into a period of "rise" and "decline." The term *decline* should *not* imply that aggregate or per capita real GNP is falling. Rather, as is evident from the last column of Table 3.1, the growth rate of per capita real GNP during a period of "decline," though positive, is lower than in the period designated "rise." The first three waves' dates are from Kondratieff, except the end date of the third wave (1938–45), which is the author's dating. The fourth and fifth waves in the table are also the author's dating.

FIRST WAVE

Rise—1790 to 1810–17[3] (Independence)

Commodity prices went through three stages during this period. (1) From 1790 to 1800, commodity prices increased by about 3 percent annually; (2) from 1800 to 1810 the annual rate of increase was about 1 percent; (3) from 1810 to 1814, commodity prices increased by about 7 percent annually. For the entire period 1790 to 1814, commodity prices increased by 6.3 percent annually. Variations in commodity prices in the United States are closely synchronized with those of England and France, as is evident from Kondratieff's data.

The period between 1793 and 1808 is characterized by North as follows:

The years 1793–1808 were years of unparalleled prosperity. True this was a hectic era, and the prosperity was interrupted on two occasions—1797–1798 and the Twenty Month Peace of Amiens 1801–1803—by the external forces which had created it. Yet the evidence suggests that this period was a high water mark in individual well-being which was to stand for many years and laid important foundations for the growth after 1815.[4]

Martin, using data which are crude and somewhat controversial, indicates that from 1799 to 1829 real per capita income rose at a rapid rate. Reflecting the buoyant economy, sailors' nominal wages rose from $8 to $30 a month between 1789 and 1810, an increase of 275 percent. Since prices increased by about 47 percent during this same period, real wages increased by 228 percent, or about 3 percent annually.

The new federal government was hardly organized before the Napoleonic wars (1793–1815) broke out and brought new markets to American shipping, shipbuilding, and agriculture. (There are many illustrations of neutral nations benefitting from wars beyond their boundaries. Neutral Japan experienced a high rate of growth during the Korean War period because of the increased demand by the United States.) It was also during this period that we witnessed the birth of the Industrial Revolution. Between 1793 and 1808 exports increased fivefold. Parallel to this, the merchant fleet registered for foreign trade jumped from 123,893 tons to 981,017 tons from 1789 to 1810. Certainly a major cause for the growth of the merchant fleet was that the European nations were preoccupied with war. Another important cause for the growth of the merchant fleet was the sympathetic support of the federal government.

The Act of July 4, 1789 reduced the tariff duty by 10 percent on imports brought into the country by American-owned and -built ships. The act also encouraged trade with the Far East by reducing the tariff on tea imported directly by American ships. At the same time it placed higher duties on tea imported from Europe, even if American ships were used. The Act of July 20, 1789 established differential duties on a ship's tonnage. A duty of 6 cents a ton was imposed on American-built ships upon entering an American port; 30 cents a ton was charged on American-built ships owned by foreigners; and 50 cents a ton was imposed on foreign-built and -owned ships. Shipbuilding activity was in an ebullient state, as illustrated by the fact that between 1789 and 1812 200,000 tons of American-built ships were sold to foreigners. The Americans, having thrown off the incubus of English mercantilism, applied some of the same mercantilistic tricks themselves. And it apparently worked to produce prosperity, at least in the short run.

With little lag behind their British cousins, the United States experienced the start of the Industrial Revolution during this period. A series of innovations in the English textile industry took place which displaced hand labor with machine power. This lowered the price of textiles significantly and increased the quantity demanded. This, in turn, increased the demand for cotton, with the result that American farmers in the South shifted from tobacco growing to cotton growing. These changes in the cotton economy and the bottleneck in the ginning of cotton led Eli Whitney to invent the cotton gin in 1793. Whitney (and Simeon North) also applied the principle of standardization and interchangeability of parts in the production of firearms in 1807. And in 1790 Samuel Slater set up the first cotton-spinning factory at Pawtucket, Rhode Island, which utilized a machine process.

Decline—1810–17 to 1844–51 (The Era of Good Feeling)

As night follows day, a period of "decline" followed a period of "rise." This period was punctuated by serious depressions (1819 and 1837), with about one-third of the period experiencing the declining phase of the short-term cycle.

In England and France the price level and nominal interest rates fell. Real interest rates probably exceeded nominal interest rates. Between 1815 and 1851, the wholesale price level fell by about 1.8 percent annually in the United States. We do not know what happened to nominal interest rates in the United States, because a continuous time series of nominal interest rates is not available.

During this period the constraints of monetary and fiscal policy by the *federal* government were relatively tight. Monetary policy during about one-third of this period was dominated by the United States Bank. The first United States Bank was established with a 20-year charter in 1791. Its central purpose in fact was to act as a central bank by regulating the money supply. By refusing to accept state bank notes unless they were backed by specie, the United States Bank placed a limit on the money supply. However, with bitter opposition coming from the agrarian and debtor interests of the West, the charter was not renewed and the bank went out of existence in 1811.

The United States Bank put a brake on inflation with its control of the money supply. With its demise, bank notes doubled between 1811 and 1816, growing by 120 percent over the entire period. Another source of inflation was related to the War of 1812, when American markets were cut off from Europe. Not unexpectedly, the price level rose to its highest level in 1815, precipitating the panic of 1819.

The second United States Bank was given a charter in 1816, again for 20 years. In 1818 the bank curtailed credit, with the inevitable consequence being the panic of 1819. At the heart of the panic and subsequent depression was the fact that many individuals bought land with inflationary expectations. When deflation took place, these expectations were disappointed and a wave of default occurred. As the main creditor, the United States Bank became the owner of large amounts of Western real estate. Hard times persisted until 1824.

The second United States Bank—Andrew Jackson's "monster"—dominated monetary policy from 1816 to 1836. Like the first United States Bank, it restrained the growth of the money supply by forcing state bank notes out of circulation. The bank was intensely disliked by westerners and southerners. In the election of 1832, the victory of Jackson and the Democrats doomed the bank. In fact, Jackson ensured the demise of the bank even before its scheduled end by removing government deposits from the United States Bank and putting them into selected state banks. Between 1836 and 1914, the United States lived without a central bank.

Fiscal policy was decidedly tight, with the federal government running a surplus of $28 million in 1835—a surplus which resulted from large revenues the federal government received from the sale of western lands. In 1836 the federal government decided to distribute the surplus to the states. This early version of revenue sharing occurred because the surplus could not be used to retire the national debt, since the federal government was out of debt from 1835 to 1837—the only time in U.S. history!

With the United States Bank out of the way, state banks increased the money supply at a rapid rate. Concurrently, *state* governments had an easy fiscal policy, borrowing money to support the mania for internal improvements. The stage was set for the depression of 1837, a depression that lasted for four to six years. The main internal improvements undertaken by the states were for canals and roads, with many of the projects of questionable value. Complicating matters was a serious crop failure in 1835. The speculative bubble in land burst when President Jackson issued an order requiring that the payment for the purchase of public land be made in specie. By the middle of 1837 every bank suspended specie payment. During the depression the bank note circulation fell from $149 million in 1837 to $58 million in 1841. Six state governments repudiated their debts.

The leading innovations, dominating and shaping the business cycle, were canal building and the expansion of the frontier with the westward movement. In the United States, canal building had its inception in the 1780s. The great era of canal building really began with the building of the 363-mile Erie Canal. The Erie Canal was an immediate success. It cut rates for bulk cargo from Buffalo to New York City from $100 to $15 per ton, and cut travel time from 20 to 8 days. New York City took on a new life and displaced other cities as the leading seaport. The success of the Erie Canal triggered a frenzy of canal building. Unfortunately, many of the canal projects had excessive costs relative to expected benefits. This era of canal building and its subsequent failure was the major factor causing the downturn in the economy in 1837.

Agricultural development centered on the existence of unoccupied land, which was readily accessible because of a liberal land policy by the federal government. A series of laws in 1785, 1800, and 1820 offered land to farmers at extremely low prices. For example, the 1800 law permitted one to purchase 320 acres or more at $2 an acre. Innovations in agriculture occurred, but at a slow rate. Because of the relative scarcity of labor, most of the innovations were labor-saving. During this period, the metal plow (1825) and the mowing machine (1831) came into use.

SECOND WAVE

Rise—1844–51 to 1866 (Manifest Destiny)

Recovering from the depression of 1837, remarkable growth apparently was underway by the early 1840s. Between 1845 and 1865, the price level rose at the rate of 3.2 percent annually. This rise occurred because of the fortuitous discovery of gold in California in 1848 and the issue of greenbacks during the Civil War. Kondratieff's data show that nominal interest rates rose in England and France. Data on nominal interest rates in the United States are not available for this period.

The principal sources of the surge in economic activity experienced during this period were the accelerated westward movement (and its concomitant conflict between the North and the South over the question of slavery) and a series of innovations in transportation, agriculture, and manufacturing. Railroad building expanded rapidly, along with the newly established manufacturing firms. From 1838 to 1860, railroad track mileage construction increased at the very rapid rate of 13 percent annually. From 1844 to 1856, the growth or railroad mileage was above the trend for the entire 1831 to 1910 period. Such a rate of increase could not be sustained, and was temporarily halted by the panic of 1857. This was the third great depression in U.S. economic history. Fortunately, the depression (though severe) was short. It was the first clear-cut depression with international dimensions. Railroad construction—a major cause of the depression of 1857—was often quite speculative and was undertaken with uncertain results. One observer characterized these excesses as follows:

Premature railroads at the West had fostered premature cities, teeming with premature traffic for premature population.[5]

The Industrial Revolution became firmly established during this period. In the 1840s there was intense competition between steam power and water power. This was particularly true in New England, where the demand for water power grew rapidly relative to a limited supply. This resulted in steam-based methods of power becoming more widespread.

Factories supplanted the home as a place of work. Cotton manufacturing flourished. Between 1840 and 1860, cotton output *increased* by 345 percent, or 7.5 percent annually. During this same period the number of cotton mills *decreased* from 1,369 to 1,091. The size of woolen factories apparently also increased during this period with the number of woolen factories increasing by 35 percent while the number of employees increased by 128 percent.

This was a golden age of invention and innovation. From 1790 to 1811, 77 patents were reported annually by the Patent Office. Between 1840 and 1850, 6,480 patents were issued and between 1850 and 1860 28,000 patents were issued. Among the more important inventions which gained increasing acceptance during this period were the introduction of coke in the production of iron in the late 1830s, Cyrus McCormick's reaper, Elias Howe's sewing machine, and Samuel Morse's telegraph. It is of some interest to ask: Why was diffusion of agricultural innovations so slow in the nineteenth century compared with the present? For example, Cyrus McCormick patented his reaper in 1834. By 1850, only 3,400 machines had been sold. By 1860, 80,000 machines had been sold. Among the reasons cited for the slow rate of diffusion of the reaper were: (1) The reaper required flat terrain, and had to wait until midwestern agriculture was established by the westward movement; (2) high real interest rates inhibited investment in the reaper; (3) low grain prices also restrained investment in the reaper. (We shall say more about the speed of diffusion below.) In any event, technological change was a powerful handmaiden for economic progress during this period.

Decline—1867 to 1890–96 (The Gilded Age)

This period was a time of political and economic turbulence. Per capita real income between 1869 and 1878 averaged $531, about one-seventh of current per capita real income. (See Table 3.1.) Between 1867 and 1890 nominal interest rates, as measured by commercial paper rates in New York City, fell steadily from about 7.4 percent to 5.4 percent. At the same time, the price level fell by almost 1 percent annually. With nominal interest rates falling more slowly than the price level, it is evident that real interest rates exceeded nominal interest rates. The period is characterized by two serious depressions, the continued "railroadization" of the United States, and a difficult time for farmers because of a falling price level.

Before proceeding further, we should note the impact of the Civil War on the postbellum period. American historians, such as Charles Beard and Louis Hacker, have claimed that the Civil War was an important stimulus to economic growth. The opposite appears to be true. There were about 600,000 casualties (about 2 percent of the population!) on both sides of the Civil War— an enormous loss of human capital to the economy, considering the average age of the soldiers. Growth rates immediately preceding the Civil War were significantly higher than those in the period immediately following it. The South was devastated. Per capita commodity output in 1880 in the South was still 21 percent below the level of 1860. The stagnation of the South is further evidenced by the fact that per capita output in 1900 was significantly below the 1859 level.

In spite of substantial agricultural growth, with acreage under cultivation increasing with the westward movement, the period was one of unrest and uncertainty for the farmer. During the Civil War prices increased rapidly. In the flush of this prosperity many farmers expanded their investment in land and equipment, thereby creating a large debtor class. When prices declined after the Civil War, the debt burden on the farmer increased further. It was only after the depression of 1893 that the price level began to rise, alleviating conditions in agriculture.

Hard times in agriculture merely slowed the technological revolution. Improved reapers, machinery for planting and cultivating, and improved plows and machines for shelling corn came into general use. The result of these technological advances was to increase the productivity per worker and to reduce the number of workers required in agriculture. From 1880 to 1900, the man-hours required to produce 100 bushels of wheat, corn, and cotton fell 29, 25, and 7 percent, respectively. At the same time, output *per acre* remained constant. On the negative side, these technological advances increased the number of landless agricultural workers.

Complementing these technological advances were developments in institutions whose goal was to increase human capital. The Morrill Act of 1862 provided subsidies from the sale of land to provide instruction in agricultural and mechanical arts. The Hatch Act of 1886 provided funds for the establishment of experimental stations in various state colleges.

During this period the Industrial Revolution became a permanent feature of the American economic landscape. The Civil War provided great stimulus to manufacturing—at least in the North. The number of wage earners increased by 56 percent over the decade of the 1860s. However, two relatively severe depressions of 1873 and 1893 perceptibly slowed economic development.

The steel industry is a vivid example of Schumpeter's "gale of creative destruction," with new inputs and outputs displacing old ones. The Bessemer process was first used in Michigan in 1856. Steel output eventually exceeded iron output. (Steel rails sold for $173 a ton in 1873 and $17 a ton by 1893. Steel rails were extremely important in the development of safer rails and permitted increased speeds by trains.) The Bessemer process was displaced by the open hearth method, and by 1910 open hearth steel production exceeded Bessemer steel production.

Shoemaking was revolutionized by adapting Howe's sewing machine to the sewing of uppers. McKay innovated a similar machine for sewing the uppers onto the sole. In 1832, Egberts successfully applied power to the knitting of hosiery. As a result, manufacture of hosiery shifted from the home to the factory in the post-Civil War period.

Schumpeter emphasized that innovative waves are required to offset the older nongrowing industries if we are to have positive growth rates. Expansion of the railroad and steel industries was central to producing a new innovative wave. Railroad mileage grew at the rate of 5.2 percent annually from 1867 to 1896. Railroad construction investment was both a cause and an effect of economic activity. There is little doubt that the speculative excesses associated with railroad construction were a major cause of the depressions of 1873 and 1893. On the other hand, it is also clear that the depressions of 1873 and 1893 slowed the growth rate of railroad construction.

Railroad enterprisers were viewed by many as fat cats, operating with little moral constraint, for example, the Credit Mobilier of 1867 which involved bribes to congressmen and Jay Gould's notorious watering of railroad stock. Much of the opposition to the railroads came from the Granger Movement. The main point of the Granger Movement was to control the perceived monopoly power of the railroads. Eventually, this led to the enactment of many state laws to limit the power of railroad management and eventually led to the enactment of the Interstate Commerce Law of 1887, which established the ICC.

The National Bank Acts of 1863 and 1865 put the federal government in control of the currency. It provided for reserve requirements for the newly established national banks. In addition, a 10 percent tax was levied on state bank note issues, effectively driving them out of circulation.

During this period there were continuous efforts by the agrarian interests to increase the money supply in order to raise the price level, thereby alleviating the debt burden of farmers. Agricultural prices declined from the mid–1860s to the mid–1890s. Such efforts to increase the money supply eventually led to the Bland-Allison Act of 1878 and the Sherman Silver Purchase Act of 1890. Both acts authorized the federal government to buy silver and increase the amount of silver coin or treasury notes in circulation.

This period was marked by two severe depressions. Large investments by railroad companies to build the 30,000 miles of track between the years 1867 and 1873 produced negligible profits. In addition, the opening up of western lands decreased land values in the older settled areas, producing financial distress for many farmers. It all came to a head when Jay Cooke & Company, the largest brokerage firm engaged in the building of the Northern Pacific, failed. This produced the panic of 1873. The depression of 1873 lasted for several years, and was the most severe to date.

Similar to the depression of 1873, railroad investment was very speculative, and these excesses were in the forefront of the cause of the depression of 1893. A complicating factor was the attempt to maintain the gold standard by demanding the repeal of the Sherman Silver Purchase Act of 1890. Following the 1893 panic, 153 railroad companies filed for bankruptcy.

The second Kondratieff wave from 1844 to 1896 illustrates vividly the link between the short business cycle and the long Kondratieff cycle. Jonathan Hughes puts this well:

The long-term growth path is produced by the algebraic sum of the ups and downs of the shorter-term business cycles. In expansions, extra entrepreneurial force is released by a wave of optimism, by growing markets, high profits, rising prices, easier access to finance. In cyclical downswings only the most efficient survive.... (It) was hard and ruthless, and, Schumpeter argues, effective in the creation of economic growth by unimaginable dimensions. The great growth period 1842–96 (trough to trough) was a Kondratieff cycle.... Schumpeter called it "the bourgeois Kondratieff" because it saw vast industrialization all over the commercial world as well as in the United States.[6]

THIRD WAVE

Rise—1890–96 to 1914–20 (Dollar Diplomacy)

During this period there was relatively rapid expansion. This is apparent from the 1.7 percent annual growth rate of per capita real income. (See Table 3.1.) Between 1898 and 1914, interest rates, as measured by New York City commercial paper rates, rose from 3.25 to 4.53 percent. This is consistent with Kondratieff's data, which show a general rise in nominal interest rates in England and France. The Federal Reserve cost-of-living index increased by 1.8 percent annually. Again, this is consistent with Kondratieff's data.

Business was stimulated by a series of good harvests, greater exports, and a series of very important innovations. The prosperity of this period was interrupted by the panic of 1907, which was brief but severe. The fundamental cause of the panic was speculation and overexpansion by the larger banks. The panic began when the Knickerbocker Trust Company closed its doors to prevent a run on the bank. This in turn was a disaster for many of the speculative ventures which involved investments in the new innovations. The panic of 1907 demonstrated the defect of the national banking system. While the system provided a national currency, it was prevented from varying the amount of money sufficiently to meet seasonal and other sudden demands on the currency. This dissatisfaction with the national banking system led to the establishment of the Federal Reserve system in 1913.

At the beginning of this period, several significant innovations occurred to set the stage for a restructuring of the economy. As Conrad says:

In each case the expansion (of each innovation) was rapid and together were no doubt sufficient to make the recovery after the depression of 1893 carry on to become the upswing of the third Kondratieff.[7]

Among the major innovations were the telephone, the electric street car, and electric light and power. These innovations had their main impact on this period, even though as inventions they are typically dated in the late nineteenth century.

American imperialism of this period had a significant impact on the economy. The external expansion of the United States appears to be a natural sequel to "manifest destiny" and the internal westward expansion which was coming to a close. The imperialism was caused by economic conditions associated with the Industrial Revolution. Not only did new territories provide new markets, but they also provided an outlet for investment and were a source of raw materials. The Spanish-American war found the United States essentially in possession of Cuba, the Philippines, Puerto Rico, and Guam. Economic control and the presence of the marines had for all practical purposes made Panama, Nicaragua, the Dominican Republic, and Haiti American protectorates. Parallel to the control of these areas went an increase in U.S. exports and investment. For example, American investment amounted to $50 million in Cuba in 1898, and American exports amounted to $100 million annually.

Decline—1914–20 to 1938–45 (Boom and Bust)

During this period, per capita real income grew at 0.6 percent annually—much lower than the previous period's rate of 1.7 percent annually. Over the entire period 1914 to 1938 the consumer price index rose 1.4 percent annually. However, this masks the fact that the consumer price index was quite unstable over shorter periods. For the periods 1914–20, 1920–22, 1923–29, 1929–33, and 1933–38 the price level changed at an annual percentage rate of 3.3, −10.0, 1.0, −7.0, and 2.6, respectively. Nominal interest rates (using commercial paper rates in New York City) between 1914 and 1938 fell from 4.5 percent to the exceptionally low level of 1.0 percent by 1938—except for increases in the late 1920s and the World War II period.

During World War I, prices and wages rose and business prospered. This was followed by the depression of 1920–21. Exports, which had soared during World War I, fell precipitously by 1921. The fall in real disposable income reduced consumption expenditures. With the onset of the depression, many farm prices decreased by about 50 percent. Unemployment in 1921 was 11.9 percent. By the end of 1922 the severe deflation had run its course and adjustments were made to the lower price level.

From 1923 to 1929, dubbed the "Roaring Twenties," the American people experienced prosperity, with the major exception of agriculture. Monetary and fiscal policy were surprisingly tight. From 1923 to 1929, the money supply grew by 2.6 percent annually and the federal government's budget was in surplus in every year—a surplus averaging about 1 percent of GNP.

Innovations in this period mainly took the form of new durable consumer goods. The major innovation was the automobile and the truck. From 1914 to 1929 there was a fivefold increase in motor vehicle registrations. The increase in the number of automobiles and trucks led to a large increase in road construction. Other consumer goods such as the radio and the refrigerator became common possessions of the consumer. In this period the motion picture industry experienced a "takeoff." That great American financial innovation of buying "on time" took root, with about 15 percent of consumption being supported by credit by the end of the 1920s. A significant innovation occurred in retailing, with the growth of chain stores offering goods at discount prices. Finally, the consumption binge was supported by the wealth effect associated with the bull market on Wall Street.

In the 1920s the United States shifted from a debtor to a creditor nation. In 1914 the United States was a net debtor to the rest of the world to the tune of $3 billion. By 1933 the United States was a net creditor of $20.6 billion. Many of the investments took the form of American corporations expanding internationally, setting up plants overseas or buying up foreign facilities.

Between 1923 and 1929 common stock prices increased by 205 percent! It all came to a head with the October 29, 1929 stock market crash. So began the descent into the Great Depression. Between 1929 and 1933 manufacturing output was cut in half. The GNP fell by 25 percent. By 1933, unemployment officially was about 22 percent. Unemployment rates were about 4 to 5 percentage points lower if we count those on government make-work schemes as employed. However, unemployment rates by owners of small businesses, not reflected in the official unemployment data, would raise the unemployment rate.

Government policy exacerbated the situation. The Smoot-Hawley tariff was passed. The Smoot-Hawley tariff was the highest in American history and made it all but impossible for the rest of the world to export to the United States in order to pay its debts to the United States. The Federal Reserve tightened the nominal money supply, thereby contributing to the financial crisis; that is, the Federal Reserve failed to offset the loss of reserves stemming from a currency drain.

Though the Hoover administration had attempted to stay the decline by such measures as the establishment of the RFC, price supports for farmers, and a modest public works program, the decline continued to 1933. By 1933 the banking system was in a state of collapse. The incoming Roosevelt administration, after declaring a bank holiday, restored the banking system to stability with the establishment of the Federal Deposit Insurance Corporation (FDIC). Among other important measures adopted by the Roosevelt administration were an expanded public works program, price supports for agriculture, the Wagner Act, and the Social Security Act.

Yet recovery was slow. The official unemployment rate fell from 24.9 to 19 percent between 1933 and 1938. The reasons for the slow recovery are not difficult to find. From 1933 to 1938, monetary and fiscal policies were tight. Demand deposits, after being decreased by 66 percent between 1929 and 1933, were increased by a mere 35 percent between 1933 and 1938. (Excess legal reserves persisted to 1938 so that if the banks were all "loaned up" with zero excess legal reserves the money supply would have grown faster. But apparently there was insufficient demand for loans during this period.) Fiscal policy was also tight, even though there were significant federal government deficits from 1933 to 1938. These deficits were mainly the result of the decline in the economy; that is, when national income fell, tax revenues decreased relative to government expenditures. If the economy had been at full employment, the Roosevelt administration would have experienced a surplus in the federal government budget; that is, when national income rises, tax revenues increase faster than government expenditures. To rub salt in the wounds of the economy, tax rates were increased in 1935 and in 1937, contributing to the depressed state of the economy in 1937. With the advent of World War II there was a complete turnaround in public policy. The money supply increased rapidly and larger deficits were incurred. And, as expected, unemployment disappeared and national income increased significantly.

FOURTH WAVE

Rise—1938–45 to 1969 (The American Challenge)

We shall be relatively brief in discussing the fourth wave because we shall refer again to this period in future chapters.

As shown in Table 3.1, during this period real per capita income rose by 2.6 percent annually—the highest growth rate of any previous period. This is to some extent the result of taking 1938 as our base year—a year of significant unemployment. However, if we take the period from 1946, a year of full employment, to 1969 the per capita real income growth rate is still high, equal to 2.1 percent annually. (See Table 3.2.) Note that the fourth wave's "rise" rate of income growth is higher than the third wave's "rise" rate; this is also true when we compare the fourth and third waves' periods of "decline." It suggests that per capita income growth rates may have a very long-run rising trend. We cannot be certain since we are observing only about 100 years of data.

The price level (i.e., the GNP deflator) increased by 3.1 percent annually between 1946 and 1969, with the largest increases coming in the immediate postwar period and the Korean War period. Nominal interest rates (i.e., three-month Treasury bills) rose steadily from 2 percent in the mid–1950s to over 6 percent by 1969. Pro-

Table 3.2

**Post-World War II Indicators of the Performance of the U.S. Economy—
Annual Percentage Changes**

	Real GNP	Real GNP Per Capita	Price Level (GNP deflator)	Output Per Hour
1946–1969	3.2	2.1	3.1	3.0[a]
1970–1987	2.6	1.6	5.6	1.3

Source: Computed from data in Economic Report of the President for 1988.

[a]Initial year 1947, the first year when data are available.

ductivity, as measured by output per hour, increased at the healthy rate of 3 percent annually between 1947 and 1969.

The United States emerged from World War II as the economic giant of the world. During this period it was common to speak of the "American century" and the "American challenge." During about half the period from 1938 to 1969, the economy was more or less affected by wartime conditions.

But wars were not the only factor keeping the economy tight. More important was a stream of innovations which changed the economy in a fundamental way and led to a high rate of investment. Among these innovations were electronics, the computer, air transport (along with airport construction), superhighway construction, the materials revolution, and the green revolution.

During this period the volume of international trade expanded rapidly, with the dollar becoming the key currency. Many factors caused this resurgence in the international economy. Following World War II, the United States extended foreign aid to former allies and enemies alike. In addition to this, the newly established International Monetary Fund and the World Bank were effective in keeping exchange rates reasonably stable and in stimulating economic development. And the operation of GATT was successful in decreasing international trade barriers. As a result the world witnessed what the media dubbed the "German miracle," the "Italian miracle," the "Japanese miracle," and so forth.

In the 1950s the United States experienced two brief recessions

(1953 and 1958). The 1960s was a period free of recession. In 1964, large tax cuts succeeded in driving unemployment rates below 4 percent. By the late 1960s, public expenditures were increasing rapidly because of the double commitment to the war on poverty and the war in Viet Nam. Tax rates were increased by 10 percent, but unfortunately failed to halt the inflationary threat because the tax increase was delayed by political conflict between the president and the Congress.

It should be noted that all innovations do not necessarily emanate from the private economy. The GI bill, which subsidized World War II veterans' education, was extremely important in expanding the stock of human capital. Furthermore, in spite of all its short-comings, the application of Keynesian countercyclical finance on net balance probably helped to stabilize the economy at a fairly low level of unemployment.

Decline—1970 to 1990–92 (Productivity Malaise)

From 1970 to 1987 the growth rate of per capita real income dipped to 1.6 percent annually. (See Table 3.2.) From 1970 to 1987, the price level (i.e., the GNP deflator) increased by 5.6 percent annually. Over the entire period nominal interest rates (i.e., three-month Treasury bills) did not change much, except for the double-digit interest rates from 1979 to 1982.

This period is not without significant innovations. Among the more important innovations are electronics (TV and VCR), the computer (supercomputers, micro and personal computers, and the word processor), robotics, and space exploration. Yet a nagging question persists: Why did productivity, as measured by the rate of increase in output per labor hour, fall from 3.0 percent for the period 1947 to 1969 to 1.3 percent for the period 1970 to 1987? (See Table 3.2.) Economists have offered a variety of answers to this question. The most important are: (1) Savings and investment rates have fallen; (2) the quality of our educational institutions has declined, particularly with regard to science and mathematics; (3) loss of the work ethic; (4) excessive governmental regulation, such as environmental controls; (5) research and development expenditures relative to sales have fallen; (6) excessively high rates of taxation; (7) the worldwide energy price increases that took place in 1973 and 1979; (8) it is a statistical fiction.

Point 8 is exploited by Michael Darby to explain the productivity decline. He points out that the raw data should not be used to compare productivity over time. Darby shows that the composition of the labor force changed in the 1970s so that there was a disproportionate increase in workers who were new immigrants, female, and young. These workers have below-average productivity, thereby reducing the overall rate of productivity increase during this period. He concludes that

... there has been no substantial variation in secular U.S. labor productivity growth after adjustment for demographic trends.[8]

Darby makes an important point, but exaggerates the importance of the statistical problem. The other factors (points 1 to 7) were at work to diminish the productivity rate. The savings and investment rates have fallen; research and development expenditures relative to sales have fallen; and the quality of the U.S. educational system has suffered. One would expect these changes to lower the rate of increase in productivity—a point that Darby does not challenge directly.

Linked to the productivity problem was the decline in the manufacturing sector, particularly steel and autos, as well as electronics, shoes, and textiles. American steel output went into a steep decline. American steel output as a percentage of world output was 47.0, 20.1, and 15.5 percent in 1950, 1970, and 1981 respectively. American steel producers suffered a technological lag, maintaining obsolete open hearth facilities in production. The automobile industry failed to respond to a change in consumer demand. The demand for smaller automobiles increased when OPEC quadrupled the price of crude oil in 1973. The American automobile producers, believing that the change was temporary, made no basic changes in their products, merely offering the down-sized version of extant models.

Unfortunately, they were wrong that the OPEC cartel would be short-lived (as were the majority of economists, including the author). The failure of the steel and auto industries have common characteristics which contributed to their decline, besides the factors mentioned above: (1) In the 1950s both industries had little market competition and operated as tight oligopolists; (2) there was negligible competition internationally; (3) both industries were highly unionized. The net result of this industrial structure was above-average profits for the producers and compensation of workers that exceeded the competitive level. With the revival of industry in Europe and Japan, the halcyon days for the American steel and auto producers were numbered. Success breeds failure!

The productivity slowdown had its impact on inflation. In the early 1970s the Nixon administration experienced inflation in the 5 to 6 percentage range annually, the legacy of the Viet Nam war. In 1970, price controls were imposed on the American economy which only made the situation worse. The Nixon administration in 1971 also closed the gold window, effectively letting the dollar float, putting an end to Bretton Woods. The Ford and Carter administrations were preoccupied with adjusting to the increase in the price of oil. The Carter administration had solemnly promised to balance the federal government budget, a pledge that haunted the administration. By the end of the Carter years the misery index (the unemployment rate plus the rate of inflation) was at record levels.

During the Reagan administration the clarion call was "supply-side" economics. Supply-siders believed that cuts in tax rates would increase output by increasing the incentive to save and invest and increasing the will to work. Many supply-siders also argued that the high marginal tax rates were largely responsible for the decline in the rate of increase of productivity because the high tax rates discouraged work and savings. Further, it was held that cuts in tax rates would be self-financing, because the reduction in government revenues associated with a cut in tax rates will at least be offset in time by the increased revenues caused by the larger tax base resulting from larger output. Most economists remained skeptical.

Supply-side economics was given a test of sorts during the early Reagan years. Tax rates were significantly cut in 1981. In addition, federal government expenditures increased faster than GNP between 1980 and 1987. Concurrently, the Federal Reserve administered a tight money policy in a determined effort to reduce double-digit inflation. The result of this policy was to significantly increase the federal government's deficit, contrary to the more optimistic expectations of supply-siders. The combination of a tight monetary policy and an easy fiscal policy also increased the international value of the dollar to new heights, with the deficit in the balance of trade expanding rapidly. The personal savings rate did not increase as supply-siders expected—though this result might be accounted for by the bull market in stocks that began in the early 1980s. The years 1980 to 1982 were years of double-digit unemployment. From 1982 to 1988 the economy experienced the longest post-World War II economic expansion. In retrospect, one can say that the demand-side effect of the large deficits in the federal government's budget increased aggregate demand and were more significant in sustaining prosperity than the intended supply-side effects intended to expand savings and investment.

Some economists have become alarmed at the increase in the debt-income ratio. It is contended that a decline in income could lead to disaster, with many households and firms defaulting on their debt obligations. Between 1970 and 1987 the debt-income ratio rose from 1.37 to 1.84—defining debt as the nominal debt of the domestic nonfinancial sector and income as nominal GNP. It is difficult to estimate the optimal debt-income ratio for the United States. If the amplitude of the business cycle grows, and the income growth rate is low, a smaller debt-income ratio is required. However, if the amplitude of the business cycle diminishes and the income growth rate increases—as we are forecasting—the increase in the debt-income ratio is not a significant problem. Furthermore, it should be pointed out that much of the additional debt is related to the one-shot but rapid development in the use of credit cards by households. In addition, because the period of mortgage loans has been increased, additional mortgage debt may not imply that monthly payments are any higher. Thus we have serious doubts that the growth of the debt-income ratio is excessive. In any event, if the growth rates were forecast in fact occur, the debt burden will be decreased. The problem of the debt burden is really the problem of achieving high and stable economic growth in disguise.

If we take the history of the fourth wave seriously, we are bound to conclude with F. Scherer:

... from the 1940s into the late 1960s there was a distinct surge of economic activity much like a Kondratieff-Schumpeter upswing (and perhaps even the first one ever!). Thereafter, (since 1968) although the evidence is far from complete, the United States entered a period that has all the earmarks of a Kondratieff-Schumpeter downswing.[9]

Let's summarize this account of the four waves. This "Cook's Tour" of American economic history is not only persuasive that long waves exist, but also that the dating that brackets each wave, as well as the periods designated "rise" and "decline" is reasonable, if not compelling. The essential underlying force for creating both the short and long cycles is waves of innovation which require large investments. The inherent characteristic of these waves of innovation are that investment comes in bunches because of the process of imitation. Once a new innovation gains some acceptance, it tends to beget imitation by others so that they can "get in on the ground floor." Take away the process of innovation and its diffusion and you take away the systemic nature of the economic cycle.

It must be emphasized that these waves of innovation are at the heart of economic progress in a market-oriented economy. On average, per capita real income is significantly higher in a given cycle compared to the previous cycle. We are now approaching a turning point in the long wave, going from "decline" to "rise." The justification for these great expectations with regard to the fifth wave is the subject matter of future chapters.

Before concluding this chapter we should take note of other economists who lend support to the concept of long waves. As was indicated above, academic economists, guardians of the "conventional wisdom," have largely ignored the ideas of the economists cited here.

Angus Maddison[10] examined long swings in economic growth. He emphasized the close international correspondence of long waves. Maddison combined the growth rates of 16 countries which he considered to be advanced capitalistic nations. These nations are the United States, the United Kingdom, Italy, Germany, Belgium, Japan, France, the Netherlands, Canada, Australia, Switzerland, Austria, Sweden, Denmark, Norway, and Finland. Table 3.3 shows the various phases of the Kondratieff long waves as Maddison sees them. Maddison's dates are strikingly close to those of Table 3.1.

Jay Forrester[11] concludes that long waves come about because the capital goods sector experiences excess capacity worldwide. This phenomenon is illustrated by the present state of the steel and automobile industry. W. W. Rostow[12] concludes that the depressed ratio of raw material prices to manufactured goods prices is the culprit causing a Kondratieff-like decline in the U.S. economy during the last two decades. Herman Kahn[13] believes that Kondratieff waves exist and result essentially from behavioral and ideological changes in the population. Edward Dewey and Edwin Dakin[14] support the concept of Kondratieff long waves by using a mathematical

Table 3.3
Maddison's Long Waves

Period	Phase	Annual Growth Rate of Real GNP
1870–1885	decline	2.5
1886–1914	rise	3.3
1914–1947	decline	1.8
1948–1973	rise	4.9
1974– ?	decline	

and somewhat mechanical approach. Economic historians such as A. Conrad[15] and J. Hughes[16] give additional support to the concept of long waves. Freeman, Clark, and Soete[17] are convinced that Kondratieff long waves are created by advances in basic science. Finally, the debate over theoretical and empirical bases for long waves is summarized in a conference held in 1985.[18]

This parade of authorities, who join Kondratieff and Schumpeter in support of long waves, can only be ignored at our own risk. Economic history is *not* forced into the Procrustean bed of Kondratieff and Schumpeter.

The time has come for us to examine the nature of the fifth wave and its period of "rise." This wave is expected to commence in the early 1990s, with per capita real income growing by *at least* 2.5 percent annually over the next two or three decades.

NOTES

1. Joseph A. Schumpeter, "The Analysis of Economic Change," *The Review of Economic Statistics* (1935). Reprinted in *Readings in Business Cycle Theory* (Philadelphia: The Blakiston Company, 1944), p. 12.

2. Nikolai D. Kondratieff, "The Long Waves in Economic Life," *The Review of Economics and Statistics* (November 1935), pp. 34–35. (This is a reprint, which first appeared in the *Archiv fur Sozialwissenschaft und Sozialpolitik* in 1926.)

3. Faulkner's excellent *American Economic History* (Harper & Row, 1931) is the main source of information used for the first three waves.

Income and price data are from *Historical Statistics of the United States, Colonial Times to 1970* (U.S. Department of Commerce, 1972), as well as from Kondratieff, "Long Waves."

4. Douglas C. North, *The Economic Growth of the United States, 1790–1860* (W. W. Norton, New York, 1966), p. 53.

5. Faulkner, *American Economic History*, p. 234.

6. Jonathan Hughes, *American Economic History*, 2nd ed. (Scott, Foresman and Co., New York, 1987), pp. 328–29.

7. Alfred H. Conrad, "Income Growth and Structural Change" in Seymour E. Harris (ed.), *American Economic History* (McGraw-Hill, New York, 1961), p. 283.

8. Michael Darby, "The U.S. Productivity Slowdown," *American Economic Review* (June 1984), p. 315.

9. F. M. Scherer, *Innovation and Growth* (MIT Press, Cambridge, MA, 1984), pp. 263–64.

10. Angus Maddison, "Phases of Capitalistic Development," *Quarterly Review, Banca Nazionale del Lavoro*, 121, June 1977.

11. Jay Forrester, "How the Long-Wave Theory May Explain the Sluggishness in Capital Formation," *Financier*, September 1977, pp. 34–38.

12. In Jay Forrester and Nathaniel Mass, "Understanding the Changing Bases of Economic Growth in the United States," *U.S. Economic Growth From 1973 to 1986* (1); U.S. Congress.

13. Herman Kahn, *World Economic Development* (Westview Press, Boulder, CO, 1979).

14. Edward Dewey and Edwin Dakin, *Cycles: The Science of Prediction* (Henry Holt, New York, 1947).

15. Conrad, "Income Growth."

16. Hughes, *American Economic History*.

17. Christopher Freeman, John Clark, and Luc Soete, *Unemployment and Technical Innovation* (Greenwood Press, New York, 1982).

18. Tibor Vasko (ed.), *The Long-Wave Debate* (Springer-Verlag, New York, 1987).

4

The Accelerating Gale of Creative Destruction

The United States is experiencing the greatest technological revolution in at least fifty years as the information and communications age spreads throughout the industrial world. . . . There is thus a very large unrealized potential from innovations already known.[1]

Americans have witnessed the permanent revolution of technological progress since the birth of the nation. The prospect for the next two or three decades can be characterized by the popular message: "You ain't seen nothin' yet." A combination of economic forces at both the micro and macro levels are expected to raise the rate of technological change, thereby raising the growth rate of real income per capita.

From this point on we will emphasize the prospective view of the economy. By their very nature, all forecasts have a speculative quality. However, some forecasts are better than others because they are evolved out of an understanding of the past and a logical view of how the economy operates. In this chapter emphasis is on underlying economic forces causing technological change without specifying particular outcomes in terms of individual inventions and innovations which are expected to take place. If we understand cause and effect we can forecast the effect by knowing that the cause is operating. For example, one can indirectly and effectively forecast the price level for a given year if one knows what has happened to the money supply in prior years. To try to forecast specific technological levels for the next two or three decades smacks of science fiction, and one must constrain the imagination. It should be noted that when reference is made to specific technologies, for example, future developments of the computer, we are speaking of technologies that already exist and are awaiting exploitation.

Before proceeding, let us discuss some preliminaries. It is essential to distinguish invention from innovation, and innovation from its diffusion. Invention is the prescription for a new product or process with the prospect of its ultimately being useful. When an invention is applied or commercialized for the first time you have an innovation. Once an innovation takes place there is the process of diffusion whereby the innovation comes into common use. The distinction between invention and innovation is somewhat hazy because the inventor and the innovator are often one and the same individual or firm; for example, DuPont invented and innovated the use of nylon. Furthermore, inventions often undergo constant modification through time, so that it is difficult to pinpoint the date of an invention. Was James Watt the inventor of the steam engine in 1776, or did he merely make some improvements in the Newcomen engine invented in 1712?

Theoretically, invention can take place at a rate which is excessive from the social point of view. However, this is unlikely because one cannot predict the results beforehand, so that it is inherently risky to attempt to invent. And, if we assume that inventors are risk-averse, the supply of invention will be reduced. Furthermore, the social net benefits exceed the private net benefits of invention because the inventor cannot appropriate all the benefits from an invention. This is particularly true for basic research. Einstein could not charge a fee for the use of $E = mc^2$. Nor could Henry Ford charge others a fee for implementing mass production techniques. Nor is it likely that the rate of innovation will be excessive from a social point of view for the same reasons that we cannot have an excessive rate of invention. Not only is innovation risky, but, like invention, not all its benefits can be appropriated by the innovator. The social return from nylon was no doubt much higher than the private return to DuPont—but the development of nylon had a high enough rate of return for DuPont to develop it without public subsidy. The rate of return on hybrid corn was 700 percent. But none of the returns from hybrid corn were received by the seed producers. Rather, consumers benefitted in the form of lower prices because entry into the hybrid-seed industry was relatively easy.[2]

Finally, it should be noted that there are product innovations and process innovations. The former involves a new product, while the latter does not. Both types of innovation increase productivity, but process innovations, which involve new ways of producing old products, are easier to measure than product innovations, which involve new products. Whether a good is a process innovation or a product innovation depends on one's vantage point. New machines are product innovations from the viewpoint of the machine goods industry, but are process innovations from the viewpoint of the consumer goods sector.

If the rate of innovation and diffusion is increased, the value of old capital will be diminished. This need not dampen the rate of investment or the rate of growth. If the rate of obsolescence increases because of higher rates of innovation and diffusion, one can expect adjustments in the marketing and investment processes. For example, firms will rent rather than buy capital, or the quality of the product will change so that the expected physical life will tend to coincide with the shorter economic life.

Let us now turn to the factors which will influence the prospects for technological advance—prospects that are remarkably bright.

NEW TECHNOLOGIES OF WIDE ADAPTABILITY ARE EXPECTED TO OCCUR

Many authorities in analyzing technological change emphasize major new technologies which are able to have a broad impact on the economic system lasting for decades. Interest is not on any particular industry or product. Rather, the focus is on clusters or constellations of related inventions and innovations. Freeman et al. believe developments in synthetic materials and electronics are examples of a new technology system. And these new technology systems are intimately related to the bandwagon effect:

The bandwagon effect is a vivid metaphor and it relates to the rapid diffusion process which occurs when it becomes evident that the basic innovations can generate super-profits and may destroy older products and processes. The big-boom phase of the post-War Kondratieff could be described as the roughly simultaneous rolling of several new technology band-wagons: for example, the computer bandwagon, the television bandwagon, the transistor bandwagon, the drugs bandwagon and the plastic bandwagon were all rolling fast in the 1950s as well as some other bandwagons like consumer durables.[3]

Which new technology systems will dominate in the next few decades is difficult to predict—though it is easier to predict broad developments than specific innovations. There is enormous potential for further innovation. It is probably no exaggeration to say that the innovation supreme has been and *will be* the computer. During the 1980s we have been passing through the computer's model T stage. In fact, the impact of the computer on the economy will probably exceed that of other major innovations such as the printing press, steam, and motor vehicles. As Freeman et al. say,

It was the innovation of the electronic computer, in combination with a whole cluster of innovations associated with solid state technology, which vastly extended the range of application of electronics in control systems, information systems and telecommunication systems. The convergence of these associated technologies was the most important development of the fourth Kondratiev and may provide one of the elements for a fifth expansionary wave. The "sum" at the center of this whole constellation of associated inventions and innovations was the electronic computer.[4]

Along with the developments associated with the computer will be developments in energy (superconductivity and fusion), biotechnology, and space, as well as a myriad of other developments. All of these technologies will be interrelated, with developments in one affecting other areas. We agree with Laudau's comment at the head of this chapter that there is "a very large unrealized potential from innovations already known."

It should be noted that, as the rate of innovation increases, the rate of investment also increases. The increased rate of investment will reduce the average age of the capital stock. Because the younger capital stock embodies the latest advances in technology, one would expect productivity to be enhanced along with the rate of economic growth.

Table 4.1
Average Time Interval from Invention to Innovation

Period	Kondratieff Phase	Average Time Interval in Years
1885–1919	Rise	37
1920–1955	Decline	24
1945–1963	Rise	14

Source: Frank Lynn, "An Investigation of the Rate of
Development and Diffusion of Technology in Our
Modern Industrial Society," Report of the National
Commission on Technology, Automation, and Economic
Progress, Washington, D.C. 1966 (Second column added)

THE LAG BETWEEN INVENTION AND INNOVATION AND DIFFUSION WILL DIMINISH

Enos[5] found that the interval between invention and innovation is diminished when the inventor is involved in the innovative process. For example, Eli Whitney was an inventor-innovator—a precursor of Thomas Edison's approach as well as that of the modern corporation. The cotton gin was invented in 1793 and within a decade was in general use. The rise of the corporate laboratory and the concomitant decline in the number of independent inventors imply that in the future we can expect a faster rate of innovation.

There is some evidence that the interval of time elapsing between invention and innovation has declined historically. Lynn[6] found that the interval of time between inventions has declined. His results are shown in Table 4.1. With the corporate laboratory becoming more dominant, there is no doubt that the lag will be shortened further. The increased degree of competitiveness from both domestic and foreign sources, as well as the improved systems of communicating ideas, will also exert pressure on firms to innovate more quickly.

It should be noted that the lag drops from 37 to 24 years between 1885 to 1919 and 1920 to 1955, a drop of 35 percent. Between 1920 to 1955 and 1945 to 1963 the lag drops from 24 to 14 years, a drop of 41 percent. The data suggest—though it is far from conclusive—that during the rising phase of the Kondratieff cycle the time interval between invention and innovation is shortened. Perhaps this further suggests that we can expect a shortening of the invention-innovation time interval during the fifth Kondratieff rising wave beginning in the 1990s.

An even more striking picture is found when one examines the speed of diffusion. Robert B. Young found that the time interval between the introduction and complete diffusion of a group of appliances has diminished significantly. Before 1920, the average span between innovation and peak production was 34 years. Among the products observed were the vacuum cleaner, the electric range, and the refrigerator. For a group of innovations that appeared in the 1939 to 1959 period, the interval of time between introduction and peak production was only eight years. Among the products observed were the electric frying pan, television, and the washer-dryer combination. The lag between innovation and complete diffusion had shrunk by 76 percent. "The post-war group demonstrated vividly the rapidly accelerating nature of the modern cycle."[7]

Further evidence of the increasing pace of innovation is illustrated by the experience of the copier and automobile industries. In the past, Xerox had a four- to five-year product cycle. But when it was found that its Japanese competitors were developing new copiers in about two years, Xerox decided to reduce its product cycle time to two years. In the automobile industry, the standard time for bringing a new model to the market was five years. By comparison, the Japanese automobile firms can design and build a new automobile in about three to four years. With Japanese competition in mind, the American automobile firms are reducing their cycle time. It is likely that current development time in the next decade will have to be cut by 25 percent and development costs by 50 percent if an automobile firm is to survive.

THE SIZE OF THE FIRM WILL INCREASE

Joseph Schumpeter in his last book, *Capitalism, Socialism and Democracy*, saw an important link between science, technology, and innovation being forged in the modern corporation. He felt that the large corporation was the carrier of the innovative process, because there was a need for large-scale financing. Also, with market power the modern corporation could be sheltered from uncertainty.

Large firms are necessary because they can reduce the amount of investment required for an innovation relative to the firm's size. One can expect the size of the firm to increase in the future because of the potential economies of scale associated with expansion. In addition, with international barriers expected to decline even further than they have in the past, the size of the firm will grow, taking on international dimensions. It should be pointed out that increasing size of firms does not imply diminished competition, since a measure of competition is the size of the firm relative to the size of the market. Thus, looking at the growing international dimensions of the market, the firm is more likely, on balance, to find itself in a more competitive situation, even though the absolute size of the individual firm increases.

Empirical evidence supports the proposition that the larger firms are more innovative than the smaller ones. Mansfield[8] concluded that between 1919 and 1958 the four largest firms in the petroleum, coal, and railroad industries carried out a greater percentage of innovations than their share of the market. The four largest steel firms, on the other hand, produced a smaller share of innovations than their market share. The reason why the steel industry is an exception to the general pattern is linked to the oligopolistic nature of steel firms, protected by price leadership in the form of "Pittsburgh Plus"—a type of pricing that accrued much more to the benefit of the largest firms in the industry than to the smaller firms. The "quiet life" is *not* conducive to innovation.

Other studies by F. Scherer, Daniel Hamburg, and John Jewkes found no evident association between the size of the firm and its scale of invention or innovative activities. Unfortunately, these studies rely on data that largely end in the 1950s. A more recent study by Soete[9] used data for the 1970s from the National Science Foundation and found support from Schumpeter's thesis. For example, he found that the largest firms in the chemical sector in the United States were research-intensive. Another study by Freeman[10] in the United Kingdom showed that the largest firms have produced a disproportionately larger share of innovation since World War II. Agriculture is an interesting example of the link between size of the firm and innovation. The average size of the agricultural firm has increased; along with this, we find that the largest farms have the highest rates of innovation. For the future the conclusion is evident:

We are likely to witness an increase in the size of the firm, which in turn will support a higher rate of innovation, thereby producing a higher rate of growth in real income.

FIRMS WILL BECOME MORE DIVERSIFIED

As firms get larger they become more diversified. This provides the firm with homemade insurance of a sort. It does not have to "put all its eggs in one basket." Rather, the modern corporation can have many research projects going on simultaneously, with expenditures on each project being small compared to the profits or net worth of the firm. Mansfield[11] emphasizes that the rate of innovation depends on the initial investment in an innovation relative to the firm's total assets.

From the perspective of the smaller firms, who are generally less diversified than the larger firms, self-insurance is not possible because of the smaller number of projects they undertake. Nor would it be possible to find an independent insurance company willing to insure a small firm against losses from invention and innovation. The very act of insurance will likely change the behavior of the firm by increasing its tolerance for losses. In addition, the firms that have higher than average risks will tend to insure, while those with lower than average risks will be reluctant to do so. The twin problems of "moral hazard" and "adverse selection" preclude making formal insurance contracts.

MARKETS WILL BECOME INCREASINGLY COMPETITIVE

Compared with the present, we can probably expect future markets to reflect a higher degree of competition. Past efforts at deregulation in such industries as trucking, banking, cable, airlines, and telephones will continue to have an impact on technological advances into the 1990s and beyond. For the future it would be no surprise if the movement toward privatization remains strong and, in fact, accelerates. There is a strong trend toward privatization for such city services as garbage collection, snow clearance, and computer services. Nor would it be surprising to see the voucher system expanded in public housing programs and to see a voucher system put in place for education. Perhaps we may see competition come to the delivery of first class mail in the United States. This impetus toward privatization will increase the degree of competition.

With the movement toward freer trade, we can expect markets to be more highly competitive. This is illustrated by the U.S.-Canadian agreement in 1987, the aim of which was to establish free trade between the two countries in manufacturing in 10 years. Consideration is also being given to a similar agreement between the United States and Mexico—thereby creating the largest free trade area in the world. Nor would it be surprising to see GATT extend its domain over trade in agriculture and services.

In a world where firms increasingly operate in markets that are workably competitive, one can expect the rate of innovation and its diffusion to increase. "...the rate of adoption in one industry might be higher than in another industry because firms in that industry...are more keenly competitive."[12] Since the best technologies are likely to be diffused more rapidly in a competitive than in an oligopolistic or monopolistic milieu, an effective policy of antitrust might be an excellent means of maintaining and increasing the rate of technological advance.

Internationalization of markets will probably reduce risk and uncertainty for the firm. Risk and uncertainty with regard to invention and innovative activity are directly related to the variability of demand for the multinational firm's product, as well as the supply of inputs. The variability of supply and demand is related to the variability of national policies on tariffs, exchange controls, and other barriers to trade. As markets become more and more internationalized, the number of markets in different nations where the firm operates will increase, decreasing risk to the firm. For example, if a firm sells in three national markets of equal size, there is greater uncertainty and risk about national policy changes than if the firm sells in 30 national markets of equal size. For example, the exclusion of Coca Cola from India and Toyota from some Asiatic countries diminished their international market share. But since both firms operate in most countries, these losses were not too serious.

This is nothing more than an application of the law of large numbers. As international markets grow, one would expect the diminution of risk and uncertainty to reduce the minimum required rate of return on invention and innovation. This, in turn, will increase the rate of innovation and productivity. The makers of the U.S. Constitution, particularly Alexander Hamilton, were aware of this problem and correctly proscribed states from interfering with interstate commerce. If each state had been a nation from colonial times to the present, there is no doubt that the rate of invention and innovation would have been lower because of the increasing uncertainty and risk. This points out the fact that risk would not vary with the number of national markets the firm operates in *if* national policies with regard to international trade were not subject to change. But since national policies, in fact, *are* subject to change, risk is related to the number of national markets in which the firm operates. Europe's technological lag behind the United States can probably be explained in part by the fact that the European market is divided into a dozen or so national markets.

IMPROVEMENT IN INFORMATION SYSTEMS WILL ACCELERATE

To the extent that information is quickly broadcast about the possibility of using innovations, the rate of innovation will be speeded. An excellent illustration of this process is the rapid spread of information by the Agricultural Extension Service of the U.S. Department of Agriculture. Information is initially received by the more progressive and larger farmers who have a better education. As the new ideas spread, less innovative farmers eventually become more receptive to the new ideas and incorporate them into their current practices.

Information systems will increasingly take on an international color. This is dramatically illustrated in the financial services industry; for example, it is extremely simple for an Australian to buy some Upjohn Company stock. From a historical perspective it is evident that the international transfer of technology is not new. Four centuries ago, Francis Bacon observed that printing, gunpowder, and the compass "changed the whole face and state of things throughout the world; the first in literature, the second in warfare, the third in navigation."[13] He failed to note that these three inventions represented successful technology transfer from China.

An interesting example of the international transfer of technology is seen in the cotton textile industry in Japan during the Meiji Period. All firms were members of the All Japan Cotton Spinners Association. As members of the association they received a trade journal which contained explicit and careful discussion of the best practices within the industry. Furthermore, one British company (Platt Brothers) provided 90 percent of the machinery, with the result that the industry was serviced by the same personnel. Thus, ideas spread quickly, the cost of information was minimal, and diffusion was quite rapid.

One would expect that under current conditions, characterized by a higher degree of education, an increase in the number of publications, and more efficient translation services, new ideas will be broadcast more quickly than in the past. Innovation and its diffusion will thereby be speeded. The current situation is characterized as follows:

Progress in technology is keeping pace with advances in scientific knowledge. Information transfer between scientist and technologist is being accelerated by new relationships in the United States between research universities and industry. Indeed, the flow of knowledge and know-how is in both directions. In the core technologies of information processing, materials, and biotechnology, the time between a scientific discovery and its commercialization can now be measured in years rather than decades.[14]

If current trends persist, we can expect to increasingly see international corporate agreements with the purpose of spreading the cost of research and exploiting the marketing potential of a large number of markets. Major industries operating in a single national market will be a thing of the past. It is inevitable that the world is becoming a "global village" when it comes to technology. The integration of technological systems internationally is illustrated by the Eureka project in Europe. Eureka is an effort to combine the best of Europe's technological capacity. The purpose is to promote and motivate cooperation between European research centers and firms. Particular emphasis is placed on artificial intelligence, supercomputers, and very fast microelectronic circuitry. Nineteen European countries have endorsed the Eureka project.

Cooperation between the United States and Japan has accelerated since 1985. The Japanese External Trade Organization reported 652 cases of joint development and technological exchange in 1985. In 1984 there were only 390 such ventures. The greatest number of joint ventures came in the high-technology sector, with 242 cases involving such products as computers, semiconductors, and integrated circuits. Not only are Japan and the United States political allies but they are also technological allies.

Another example of the international integration of technological systems is with regard to superconductivity. In 1987, Japan's Ministry of International Trade and Industry (MITI) announced plans to exploit superconductivity. The MITI has invited foreign firms to join the association that will oversee the project. The center will study applications, markets, and resources, and disseminate information on superconductivity research.

There appears to be no speed limit in the future for the spread of technological information. This is illustrated by current developments in the field of superconductivity. The Nobel committee that awards the physics prize has been characterized as cautious and slow to respond. For example, Ernst Ruska, who built the first electron microscope in 1933, had to wait until 1986 to be recognized by the Nobel committee. The work of Müller and Bednorz on superconductivity is different. They published their results of attaining superconductivity at -397 degrees Fahrenheit in a German physics journal in 1986 and were awarded the Nobel physics prize in 1987.

Beginning in 1987 there was a "take off" in efforts to raise superconductivity temperatures. At the University of Houston, Ching-Wu Chu led a group of scientists researching superconductivity. He and his colleagues raised the temperature at which superconductors lost all resistance to -293 degrees Fahrenheit. This news produced a veritable stampede. At a conference of the American Physical Society held on March 18, 1987 in New York, the central topic was superconductivity. At the start of the session on superconductivity there were 4,000 people filling a hall that had a capacity of 3,000 people. The report of the meeting made the front page of the *New York Times*.

THE AMPLITUDE OF THE BUSINESS CYCLE WILL DIMINISH

The inventor and the innovator require a minimum expected rate of return, adjusted for risk. If risk were to be decreased, the required minimum rate of return would be reduced and invention and innovation would increase. One type of risk relates to the amplitude of the business cycle. With the continued relative growth of the service sector relative to national income in the United States, the

Table 4.2
Gross National Product Per Capita Growth Rates and Their Variability

	1891–1929	1930–1949	1950–1980
Mean Percent GNP per Capita Growth Rate	1.78	1.32	2.17
Standard Deviation	6.28	9.22	2.65
Coefficient of Variation[a]	3.54	6.99	1.22

Source: Douglas A. Hibbs, Jr., The American Political Economy, Harvard University Press, 1987, p. 16.

[a]The standard deviation divided by the mean GNP per capita growth rate.

amplitude of the business cycle will diminish. Inventory fluctuations are the major source of the business cycle. However, with the relative growth of the service sector, which has no inventory problem, one can expect the amplitude of the cycle to diminish. We shall say more about the service sector in the next chapter.

There is clear evidence that business cycles are becoming less severe. Table 4.2 shows that the deviations around the mean value of GNP have decreased dramatically. From 1891 to 1929, the mean growth of per capita income was 1.78 percent, with a standard deviation of 6.28 and a coefficient of variation (standard deviation divided by the average growth rate) of 3.54. By 1950 to 1980, the mean GNP growth rate increased to 2.17 percent, while the standard deviation fell to 2.65 and the coefficient of variation fell to 1.22. The period 1930 to 1949, characterized by the Great Depression and World War II, is probably an aberration. The decline in the amplitude of the cycle is not only related to the declining importance of inventories because of the growth of the service sector, but is also probably related to the positive effect of public policies which aim to diminish the amplitude of the cycle.

Table 4.3 shows the tendency for the consumer price level to increase but for the coefficient of variation to diminish with the passage of time. Thus, if this trend with regard to the variation of the price level continues we have another source accounting for lower risk to invention and innovation. Parenthetically it should be noted that unemployment rates average 6.12 percent in the 1890 to 1929 period with a coefficient of variation of 0.66; unemployment rates averaged 5.23 in the 1950 to 1980 period with a coef-

Table 4.3
Rates of Inflation and Their Variability

	1891–1929	1930–1949	1950–1980
Mean Percent Rate of Increase in Consumer Price Level	.93	1.65	4.00
Standard Deviation	6.27	6.04	3.39
Coefficient of Variation[a]	6.74	3.66	0.85

Source: Douglas A. Hibbs, Jr., The American Political Economy, Harvard University Press, 1987, p. 21.

[a]The standard deviation divided by the mean GNP per capita growth rate.

ficient of variation of 0.27. If one were to measure economic welfare by the size of the coefficients of variation of GNP, the consumer price level, and the unemployment rate, we were clearly better off in the 1950 to 1980 period than the period 1891 to 1929.

TWO ILLUSTRATIONS

It is appropriate that we view the problems and trends discussed above from a different angle. Activity with regard to superconductivity and biotechnology illustrate many of the trends discussed above. The purpose is not to give an intensive discussion of all aspects of these two fields. Rather the purpose is to give a sense of the future in examining present activity.

Superconductivity

In 1987, the Nobel prize for physics was given to K. Alex Müller and J. Georg Bednorz of the IBM Zurich Research Laboratory for their research into superconductivity. Superconductivity is a simple idea. At low temperatures many substances lose all their resistance to the passage of electricity. However, because of the temperatures at which superconductivity takes place, the phenomenon has been difficult to use practically. Müller and Bednorz raised the superconductivity temperature to − 397 degrees Fahrenheit. Other physicists managed to push the temperature to − 280 degrees Fahrenheit.

Superconductors have currently found little application. Particle accelerators require superconductors to keep protons and neutrons moving at nearly the speed of light. In the medical field, superconducting magnets are used in magnetic resonance imaging machines—a very significant improvement over X-ray and CAT scan technology, particularly with regard to brain scans.

Benefits from the practical use of superconductivity can be enormous. A superconductivity power line could send electricity from a power plant located near a coal mine to the user with almost 100 percent efficiency so that we could have "coal by wire." A computer chip with a superconductivity connection would operate with significantly less energy, thereby increasing the ability to compute at much faster speeds. It is also possible that by a levitating magnet, trains will be able to run at about 300 miles per hour above the surface of the earth.

Industrial laboratories have been providing large sums of money to solve the superconductivity problem. President Reagan promised to loosen antitrust restrictions on intercompany cooperation. In addition, financial support from government was pledged. International competition to make superconductivity practical is intense.

A good example of governmental support is the superconductor "battery." As proposed by Professor Boom, a metallurgist and nuclear engineer at the University of Wisconsin, the $1 billion doughnut-shaped structure (20 yards thick and more than a mile in diameter) would be charged with five million kilowatts. This energy could then be released gradually during peak-load periods. The concept is known as superconducting magnetic energy storage, or SMES. The doughnut consists of a coil of superconducting electrical wire wound around a metal core; SMES is 98 percent efficient in drawing energy from the doughnut for general use. This is far more efficient than current techniques which use pump storage. Pump storage involves pumping water to a high level at night. In the day, during peak load period, the water is released to turn turbines. Pump storage is only about 70 percent efficient.

In 1987 the federal government expressed interest in the project. Two competing industrial teams were asked to design an experimental model, each being awarded $14 million in two-year contracts. The winner of this competition will then be awarded a three-year contract to construct an SMES system capable of storing at least 15,000 kilowatts of energy. The Department of Defense has also expressed interest in the project.

Many problems remain until superconductivity becomes practical. For one thing, researchers must solve the problem of making useful wires with superconducting materials, which are about as stiff as glass. In addition, it will be necessary for researchers to increase the temperature at which certain materials become superconducting.

Biotechnology

Biotechnology is expected to generate multibillions of dollars in sales. While still in the early stages of development, it is expected to bring out new products, ranging from new kinds of farm animals and plants to cancer treatments. Currently, the United States holds the lead in biotechnology, with serious challenges coming from European and Japanese firms.

Japan has invested heavily in the effort to automate reading the body's internal blueprint. Decoding genetic information involves a process known as DNA sequencing. Biologists would like to complete a catalog of the three billion pieces of genetic information found in the human DNA. Many biologists believe such a catalog would be the key to finding a cure for many diseases—a veritable revolution.

The Japanese have followed the United States and the Europeans in efforts to automate the laboratory process. Today, DNA sequencing laboratories work like automobile factories before mass production, with most of the steps being tedious routine. Scientists manually break DNA into sections, reproduce it, separate it, purify it, and repeat the process of purification. The results are put on film and analyzed visually. Automating the laboratory process would be the equivalent of introducing mass production techniques into biotechnology.

In early 1987, Walter Gilbert, Nobel laureate in biology, announced he would organize the Genome Corporation to decipher the human genome and thus reveal the biological structure of the human being's entire genetic structure. This was meant to meet the Japanese challenge head-on. It is estimated that if such an effort were successful it could result in treatment or cures for about 4,000 genetic disorders.

But firms are not waiting for the successful development of automated laboratory procedures. For example, a group of scientists at the University of Texas have reported promising results using a blood protein in treating patients with a preleukemic condition. The Immunex Corporation produced a synthetic form of the naturally occurring hormone using biotechnology.

JEREMIADS

It should be clear that we are not speaking of technological change and economic growth come hell or high water. Yet some analysts believe that technological change and economic growth are too costly because of serious side effects. This may be so, and we should examine some reasons for possibility being less optimistic. We shall be relatively brief because many of these points will be discussed again in later chapters.

The Malthusian Spector

It is not uncommon to gloomily contend that there is a natural tendency for population to grow to the limits set by the environment. Going to the wailing wall, many explain that we are running out of resources. Cheap oil will probably be gone in 100 years and coal in perhaps 300 to 500 years. But of course we will not extract oil or coal to the last drop because the extraction process will become too costly. However, a historical view of the past two centuries makes it clear that there is no constraint in sight with regard to energy or raw materials in the United States. Changes in price structure and product substitution, as well as technological advance, will continue to serve as solutions to diminished raw materials.

Malthus suggested that population grows geometrically and the food supply grows arithmetically, so that our collective destination is doomsday.[15] Fortunately, at least for the highly industrialized nations, the reverse is true: Population has tended to grow arithmetically and the food supply has tended to grow geometrically. Economic growth has slowed down the rate of increase in population. Furthermore, technological advance has more than offset the problem of diminishing returns. This is evident when we find that the price of raw materials (except for lumber) has been declining. We need not depend on starvation and misery to check population growth. The most important element is Julian Simon's "ultimate resource," the intelligence of the human being.

Future Shock

Alvin Toffler argues that the rate of technological change has accelerated, producing social stress because of the uneven rates of change in different sectors of society. This is a modern version of William Ogburn's concept of cultural lag. "Future shock" describes "the shattering stress and disorientation that we induce in individuals by subjecting them to too much change in too short a time."[16] He emphasizes that the rate and the direction of change are important. Toffler appears to be a crypto-Luddite, arguing that we should monitor technological change and slow its rate of increase.

Toffler emphasized that the rate of change is accelerating mainly due to the increased rate of technological change. Future shock and the associated angst cannot be avoided. The problem is one of finding the optimum degree of future shock. Technological advance is not a free good. The question boils down to this: Are the benefits of technological advance (higher income levels) greater than the costs (future shock as well as the foregone consumption in the present)?

Answering this question is a matter of judgment. It appears to be evident from history that nations that experience relatively high rates of technological advance and high rates of economic growth suffer less from social problems than those with low rates of technological advance and low rates of economic growth. Examples abound. The United States in the 1950s and the Japanese in the 1980s were cases where social problems appeared to be minimized—and these were periods of relatively high economic growth rates. One might cite the 1960s in the United States as a period of social instability combined with high economic growth. But its source was not the high rate of economic growth but the burgeoning civil rights movement combined with the anti-Viet Nam War movement. Social instability has many causes, with nonoptimal economic growth being only one possible cause.

The Effluent Society?

High rates of technological advance and economic growth may result in the pollution of the environment, as illustrated by the development of the steel industry. Technological advance may also decrease the level of pollution, for example, the use of modern water treatment facilities. Whether current air and water quality has deteriorated compared to 75 to 100 years ago is uncertain. One need only compare Pittsburgh around 1900 to the Pittsburgh of today to realize that the situation may be improving. Prior to the use of automobiles a serious pollution problem existed because horse droppings spread disease—particularly among youngsters who went without shoes. The automobile was thus hailed as the solution to this type of pollution, only to produce another type.

For some observers (found mostly in the middle- and upper-income brackets) the answer to the pollution problem is to have zero economic growth (ZEG) and zero population growth (ZPG). A more reasonable approach is to focus on the industries which are the main culprits: paper, food processing, chemicals, steel, and oil refining. By means of social policy we can select any level of clear air or water we desire—though it should be evident that there is a cost to maintaining clean air and water. One means of designing an effective antipollution policy is to charge firms a fee for pollution. The higher the fee the lower the rate of pollution.[17] This will, of course, increase the price of output and represents a cost. An effective antipollution policy requires some trade-off of a modest part of our standard of living for an improved environment. There is no necessary conflict between technological change, economic growth, and the desire for a clean environment.

The Poor Get Poorer and the Rich Get Richer

It is often asserted that technological change benefits the rich at the expense of the poor. Examples are given to justify this view. For example, the "Green Revolution" has been labor-saving and probably land-using, so that small farmers are made worse off, while landlords are better off. The impact on the poor is a subject of considerable controversy. The initial impact no doubt aided the higher-income farmers. However, after the initial impact there is evidence that the Green Revolution improved the economic position of the poor farmers, with labor requirements per acre rising substantially.

Selective examples over relatively short time periods will not serve as evidence linking technological change and economic growth to changes in the distribution of income. In general, empirical studies show that technological change and economic growth do not make for greater inequality and may, in fact, make for a more equal distribution of income.

It is of interest to note that during the Kondratieff fourth wave "decline" period, U.S. income distribution has become more unequal. According to the U.S. Census Bureau, between 1969 and 1986 the lowest income quintile share of money income fell from 5.6 to 4.6 percent. The share of the highest income quintile share rose from 40.6 to 43.7 percent. The main causes for these increases in inequality during this period are probably related to the large increase in the number of inexperienced young workers and the disappointing growth of productivity. These causes are expected to be largely absent beginning with the decade of the 1990s.

Technological Unemployment

Technological advance increases efficiency in production, so that the demand for inputs falls for a *given level of output*. It may decrease the demand for capital and increase the demand for labor— just so it involves *net* savings of inputs. Frequently this involves a decrease in the demand for labor, resulting in unemployment. The fear of technological unemployment has been articulated by David Ricardo, Karl Marx, and others. Norbert Wiener expressed this canard by saying that the computerization of production with automation and robotics

... will produce an unemployment situation, in comparison with which the present recession and even the depression of the thirties will seem a pleasant joke.[18]

The fear of technological unemployment is a myopic view of the economy. There is no doubt that labor displacement has taken place with regard to individual jobs, for example, printers being replaced successively by linotype and computerization. However, on the macroeconomic level there has been no net displacement of labor by the machine. This is an example of the fallacy of composition, that is, what is true for the individual is not true for the group. For the past two centuries unemployment rates have not increased in the United States in spite of the permanent revolution of more or less continuous technological change because aggregate demand has increased along with this technological change. Thus the decreased demand for labor associated with technological change has been offset by the increase in demand for labor because of increased output.

Perhaps one can understand why technological unemployment is not a serious problem for the human being by examining the "horse problem." In 1909 there were 19.7 million horses in the United States. With the continuous displacement of the horse by the motor vehicle from 1909 on, the horse population fell to 8.5 million in 1945. *If* the horse population had remained constant from 1909 to 1945, close to 50 percent of the horses would be unemployed in 1945; or, *if* there was an increase in demand for the horse offsetting the decrease in demand from technological change, there would be horse "full employment" in 1945. In fact, there was no offsetting increase in demand for horses prior to World War II, and horse "full employment" was maintained by a decrease in the horse population.[19]

Different from horses, the human being is more flexible and for the human population technological advance involves changes in types of employment rather than unemployment. To the extent that aggregate demand increases along with technological advance and there is labor mobility facilitating these changes, the problem of labor displacement by technology will be eased.

Service Sector Productivity

Baumol[20] argues that the relative growth of the service sector will tend to reduce overall productivity growth. Indirect evidence for this can be adduced if one examines price level changes in different sectors. If service sector productivity growth is lower than commodity productivity growth, the price level of the services should increase faster than that of commodities. Between 1940 and 1986, service sector prices increased 4.8 percent annually, while commodity prices increased by 4.2 percent annually. However, one should be careful to note that it is much more difficult to measure quality changes in service output than for commodity output—even though the Bureau of Labor Statistics makes an effort to adjust for quality changes, as well as new outputs. For example, a CAT scan may cost ten times that of an X-ray machine, but this does not imply that the price of examining the interior of the body has increased tenfold, since CAT scans are usually more effective as a diagnostic tool than X-rays.

Furthermore, the medical service sector price level has risen faster than the overall service sector price level. Much of this is the result of the introduction of Medicare and Medicaid and the growth of private insurance. If these programs are not significantly expanded in the future, one would expect that the medical service sector price level will rise at about the same rate as the overall price level of the service sector. Thus if one excludes the medical service sector from the overall service sector, and also takes account of the fact that the price indexes inadequately account for quality changes in the service sector, there appears to be little difference in the commodity and service sector's rates of annual price increase.

Direct evidence on productivity changes indicates that there is no significant difference in the rate of change of productivity in manufacturing and the service industries from 1945 to 1958. Between 1965 and 1979, service-producing have a higher rate of productivity increase than goods-producing industries. Between 1979 and 1985 these trends were reversed.[21] Baumol uses selective examples of low increases in productivity in the service sector, such as in education, the arts, and government services. But one can be equally selective and cite the fact that some service sectors have high rates of productivity increase. From 1929 to 1958, productivity in air transport increased at a rate of 8 to 9 percent annually—much higher than any other industry in the entire economy.[22] Thus, when one takes account of the statistical problems with price indexes and examines the direct evidence on rates of productivity change, there appears to be no significant difference in the service and manufacturing rates of productivity increase.

SUMMARY

The principal point of this chapter has been that technological change is expected to accelerate over the next two or three decades, producing a higher rate of growth in per capita income. There are many reasons for entertaining this expectation.

First, there is a wide range of new and interrelated technologies waiting to be developed. Second, the time lag between invention and innovation, as well as the time lag between innovation and its diffusion, will continue to be shortened. Third, the large firm with international connections will exploit potential economies of scale in technology. With competitive pressures from the international economy, the firm will be under pressure to innovate. Fourth, innovation will be speeded because the risks associated with it will diminish. Risk will be diminished because the firm will become more diversified and because the business cycle will be more shallow. Finally, information will be more quickly disseminated so that technological change will increase.

Many of the lamentations of woe associated with technological change are exaggerated, if not in error. Possibilities that growth will produce overpopulation or "future shock," or excess pollution, or that it will produce an excess degree of inequality are found to be misplaced. Furthermore, the growing service sector does not have a lower rate of productivity increase than the manufacturing sector.

Most of the problems associated with technological change, such as the distribution of income or pollution, can be dealt with more effectively if we have significant economic growth than if economic growth is minimal.

NOTES

1. Ralph Landau, "Technology, Economics and Public Policy" in Ralph Landau and Dale W. Jorgenson (eds.), *Technology and Economic Policy* (Cambridge, Mass.: Ballinger Publishing Co., 1986).

2. Z. Griliches, "Research Costs and Social Returns: Hybrid Corn and Related Innovations," *Journal of Political Economy*, October 1958, pp. 419–31.

3. Christopher Freeman, John Clark, and Luc Soete, *Unemployment and Technical Innovation* (Westport, Conn.: Greenwood Press, 1982), p. 67.

4. Freeman, Clark, and Soete, *Unemployment*, p. 107.

5. John Enos, "Invention and Innovation in the Petroleum Refining Industry," in *The Rate and Direction of Inventive Activity* (Princeton, N.J.: Princeton University Press, 1962), p. 309.

6. F. Lynn, "An Investigation of the Rate of Development and Dif-

fusion of Technology in Our Modern Industrial Society," *Report of the National Commission on Technology, Automation and Economic Progress* (Washington, DC, 1966).

7. Robert B. Young, "Product Growth Cycles—A Key to Growth Planning," Stanford Research Institute, undated. Cited by Alvin Toffler, *Future Shock* (New York: Bantam Books, 1970), p. 28.

8. Edwin Mansfield, *The Economics of Technological Change* (New York: W. W. Norton, 1968), pp. 109–10.

9. L. L. G. Soete, "Firm Size and Inventive Activity: the Evidence Reconsidered," *European Economic Review*, 12, 1961, pp. 319–40.

10. C. Freeman, *The Role of Small Firms in Innovation in the United Kingdom Since 1945*, Research Report No. 6, HMSO, 1971.

11. Freeman, *Role of Small Firms*, p. 120.

12. Mansfield, *Economics of Technological Change*, p. 120.

13. Francis Bacon, *The New Organon* (Bobbs-Merrill, Indianapolis, 1960), p. 118.

14. Frank Press, "Technological Competition and the Western Alliance," in Andrew J. Pierre (ed.), *A High Technology Gap? Europe, America, Japan* (New York University Press, 1987), p. 13.

15. For a modern version of the Malthusian trap see Donella H. Meadows, Dennis L. Meadows, Jorgen Randers, and William W. Behrens III, *The Limits of Growth* (New American Library, 1972), pp. 148–52.

16. Alvin Toffler, *Future Shock*, p. 2.

17. J. H. Dales, *Pollution, Property and Prices* (University of Toronto Press, 1968).

18. Norbert Wiener, *The Human Use of Human Beings* (Houghton-Mifflin, Boston, 1950), p. 189.

19. The horse population increased to 10.58 million by 1985 because demand for horses in terms of recreation increased.

20. William J. Baumol, "Macroeconomics of Unbalanced Growth: The Anatomy of Urban Crisis," *American Economic Review*, June 1967.

21. Pheobus J. Dhrymes, "A Comparison of Productivity Behavior in Manufacturing and Service Industries," *The Review of Economics and Statistics*, February 1963.

22. J. W. Kendrick, *Productivity Trends in the United States* (Columbia University Press, New York, 1973).

5

The Changing Structure of the Economy

...my more broadminded colleagues who love growth are willing to grant her only a reprieve, but not a pardon. And yet I fail to see any indications that the world is any closer now to a stationary state than it was, say, a hundred years ago. If there has been any movement at all, it must surely have been away from rather than toward it.[1]

If the economic structure is given, growth in per capita income is not possible without technological advance. However, if the economic structure changes, it is possible for the growth of per capita income to occur in the absence of technological advance. Would anyone doubt that per capita income would have grown in Lebanon in the 1980s if a reasonable degree of law and order were substituted for the chaos that in fact engulfed that tragic country sans technological advance?

As the American economy produces more service output relative to goods output, and as we witness some favorable demographic trends as well as other changes, growth will be enhanced. These changes, in combination with accelerating technological advance, underscore the sanguine forecast for the coming Kondratieff "rise." The next couple of decades will be characterized by a situation where the welfare of most individuals can be improved simultaneously. Forecasts of a zero-sum game, where GNP is more or less constant and where one person can improve his or her welfare only at the expense of others, is far off the mark.

Table 5.1
Output of Goods and Service Sectors in Billions of 1982 Dollars

	Goods	Services	Services/Goods
1929	$ 308	$ 290	.94
1987	1,655	1,781	1.08
2011[a]	`3,417	3,963	1.15
1929–1986 annual percent growth	2.9	3.2	

Source: Economic Report of the President for 1988, p. 257.

[a]Assumes goods and service sectors grow at 1929–1986 rates.

Let us turn to some of the major structural changes expected to occur in the next few decades.

THE BURGEONING SERVICE SECTOR

The service-producing sector is composed mainly of outputs from transportation, public utilities, wholesale and retail trade, finance, insurance and real estate, and government. Between 1929 and 1987, the service-producing sector grew at 3.2 percent, while the goods-producing sector grew at 2.9 percent. (See Table 5.1.) Put another way, in 1929 the service-producing sector was 94 percent of the goods-producing sector; by 1986 the service-producing sector was 108 percent of the goods-producing sector. If these growth rates continue over the next 25 years to the year 2011, the service-producing sector will be 115 percent of the goods-producing sector. These trends will change the structure and functioning of the economy in a fundamental way.

It should be noted that homework, which involves no direct money payments, is excluded from GNP. If the homework sector were included, the service sector would be much larger. To the extent that women enter the labor force and hire paid housekeepers (e.g., cooks, babysitters, professional cleaning services, day care centers), the service sector will increase relative to the goods-producing sector.

The End of the Business Cycle?

The more or less systematic swings in inventory investment during the business cycle appear to support the conclusion that anything which will stabilize inventory investment will go a long way toward stabilizing the economy. The post-World War II recessions deserve the term "inventory recessions" because disinvestment in inventory associated with forecasting errors by the firm was a major cause of these declines. It has been estimated that when 75 percent of the fluctuations in inventory investment are eliminated, the usual cycle experienced in the post-World War II period up to 1960 would be eliminated.[2]

Service sector industries have no inventory to speak of, so they do not suffer from the inventory cycles. With the growing importance of the service sector, the economy will be less susceptible to downturns. In addition, the amplitude of the business cycle has been and will be significantly reduced. From 1950 to 1986 the service sector output has never declined, with annual growth ranging from 1.4 to 14.3 percent. In contrast, the goods sector has shown an annual growth ranging from −5.0 to 11 percent (See Table 5.2.) Business cycles in the past have diminished in severity (see Table 4.2) in part because of the growth of the service sector. As time goes by we can expect the business cycle to be more and more moderate, with recessions becoming shorter and recovery periods being prolonged. Perhaps we are witnessing the slow but inevitable death of the business cycle.

Another factor reducing the severity of the business cycle is the increasing importance of the so-called economic order quantity (EOQ) model of inventory management. In this model inventory grows about half as fast as output. More precisely, we have,

$$\frac{\text{Elasticity of}}{\text{Inventory Demand}} = \frac{\text{Percent Change in Inventory}}{\text{Percent Change in Sales Volume}} = 0.5$$

For example, a 10 percent increase in sales volume will increase inventory demand by 5 percent. Put another way, the large store, such as Sears Roebuck, will have a smaller inventory relative to its sales volume than a small "mom and pop" store. Thus, even if the goods-producing sector does not decline relatively, use of the EOQ model will moderate the cycle.

Table 5.2
Goods and Service Producing Industries and Their Annual Rates of
Change, 1950 to 1986

Year	Output (Billion dollars)		Annual Change	
	Goods	Services	Goods	Services
50	561.4	470.4	--	--
51	623.6	537.7	0.109	0.143
52	641.3	567.3	0.029	0.055
53	676.6	577.6	0.055	0.018
54	643.5	579.5	-0.045	0.003
55	683.5	601.0	0.062	0.037
56	697.1	619.7	0.019	0.031
57	699.3	645.4	0.003	0.041
58	674.2	654.7	-0.035	0.014
59	716.6	681.5	0.062	0.040
60	726.8	709.9	0.014	0.041
61	730.2	743.0	0.004	0.046
62	773.5	777.0	0.059	0.045
63	797.5	811.5	0.031	0.044
64	845.2	852.8	0.059	0.050
65	904.0	891.6	0.069	0.045
66	947.7	942.7	0.048	0.057
67	993.1	990.6	0.047	0.050
68	1024.8	1032.0	0.031	0.041
69	1048.5	1066.4	0.023	0.033
70	1030.0	1092.4	-0.017	0.024
71	1037.6	1126.1	0.007	0.030
72	1093.8	1169.4	0.054	0.038
73	1175.0	1218.7	0.074	0.042
74	1159.2	1256.4	-0.013	0.030
75	1125.0	1286.4	-0.029	0.023
76	1194.7	1324.4	0.061	0.029
77	1256.2	1368.7	0.051	0.033
78	1329.1	1426.9	0.058	0.042
79	1354.6	1478.6	0.019	0.036
80	1344.2	1511.1	-0.007	0.021
81	1386.0	1533.4	0.031	0.014
82	1319.1	1547.5	-0.048	0.009
83	1367.0	1585.5	0.036	0.024
84	1503.1	1623.0	0.099	0.023
85	1533.2	1667.6	0.020	0.027
86	1569.0	1718.1	0.023	0.030

Source: Economic Report of the President, 1987, p. 253.

The implications of the growing importance of the service sector and the concomitant reduction in the amplitude of the business cycle are profound. First, one can expect employment to be more stable and bouts of unemployment for the average worker to be less frequent. In the service-producing industries, employment never decreased between 1950 and 1986. In contrast, in the goods-producing industries, employment during recession fell an average of 8 percent. This stability of employment should reduce labor costs because costs associated with excessive labor turnover and training will be reduced. Furthermore, one could expect that workers who experience steadier employment will have improved morale and will be more productive.

Second, the rate of innovation should increase. Risk will decrease because of the moderation of the business cycle. With "boom and bust" a thing of the past, the firm will be in a position to take the long view in considering new investments and innovations—a requirement particularly when one considers *major* innovations.[3] Diminished risk will also result in lower interest rates because lenders will require less of a risk premium; and diminished risk associated with the business cycle will lower the minimum acceptable rate of return required by the firm.

Third, the economic condition of the unskilled and least experienced workers should improve. These workers will have more steady employment and probably higher incomes than in the past. As unemployment rates decrease, we can expect black-worker incomes to increase faster than those of white workers, with the importance of "last in, first out" for black workers losing its significance.

CHANGING DEMOGRAPHIC PATTERNS

We showed in Table 3.2 that output per hour fell from 3 percent annually for the 1947–1969 period to 1.3 percent annually for the 1970–1987 period. Much of the decline in productivity is related to the fact that during the latter period there was a disproportionate number of workers who were young, female, or new immigrants. These workers have below-average productivity because they have less experience in the workforce. In addition, their productivity may be reduced by discrimination—a subject we will turn to below.

Since productivity is the ratio of output to employment, it is evident that using an unadjusted employment figure will be too high and will produce a downward bias in productivity. An hour of employment of a young person or a female or a new immigrant is *not* equal to an hour of employment by a native, middle-aged male. Table 5.3 shows the downward adjustments required if we are to take account of these demographic factors. The unadjusted annual growth of private employment was 2.27 percent. But when adjustments are made for age, sex, and new immigrants, the employ-

Table 5.3

The Adjusted Growth Rate for Private Employment, 1973 to 1979

	Annual Growth (Percent)
Private Employment Growth Rate	2.27
Adjustments:	
Age	- .01
Sex	- .28
New Immigrants	- .01
Adjusted Private Employment Growth Rate[a]	1.97

Source: Michael Darby, "The U.S. Productivity Slowdown", *American Economic Review*, June, 1984, p. 305.

[a]Darby also adjusts for education in his table, which we will discuss below.

ment growth rate falls by 0.3 percent—the employment growth is decreased by 0.01, 0.28, and 0.01 percent for age, sex, and new immigrants, respectively. These trends have continued into the 1980s. However, by the 1990s the labor force below the age of 35 will fall and the percentage of the labor force that is female will not be increasing. From this the future for productivity looks bright. As Darby says,

The major factor reducing productivity growth over the 1965–79 period was the increasingly youthful labor force. Now as the smaller post-pill generation enters the labor force and the baby-boom generation ages, this effect will be operating in the opposite direction to increase output per (unadjusted) hour. The sex factor may cease to slow productivity growth for either of two reasons: (1) female participation rates are approaching those of men for younger women, so the disproportionate growth of women workers may soon slow, (2) as lifetime market work becomes the norm for women, their investment in human capital should rise toward that of men.[4]

WOMEN IN THE ECONOMY

There has been a sea change in the position of women in the American economy. In fact, there has probably been more change in the status of women in the last 20 years than there has been in the last 2,000 years. These changes can be analyzed by examining employment and earnings patterns.

Employment Patterns

In the early 1900s, about 20 percent of women worked outside the home. Most of these women were single or widowed. By 1986, two-thirds of adult women worked outside the home, with the majority of these women being married. These extraordinary changes in the status of women were the result of a set of interrelated economic factors.

First, improvements in technology in the home have reduced the demand for labor in the home. In the early twentieth century, one full-time person was required to perform the household tasks. Frozen foods, dishwashers, and other mechanical contrivances have reduced the need for household labor. Second, there has been a reduction in the demand for household labor because of the very significant decline in the birth rate. Third, economic growth and the rising level of real wages in the last four or five decades have meant that women could command higher wages in the marketplace relative to the value of time spent in household work. Fourth, the nature of outside employment changed so that less physical strength was required, thereby opening up additional opportunities for women, particularly in the growing service sector. Finally, in the 1970s real wages for men fell in some years, and this probably led many women to enter the labor force to maintain family incomes.

Taxation of market wages will also affect the allocation of female labor. Other things being equal, higher tax rates during the 1960s and 1970s probably inhibited the shift from the home to the labor market for women. However, with the decline in the maximum marginal tax rate to 33 percent in the 1986 tax bill, the shift from home to the labor market by female workers will be speeded.

All of the forces cited above are expected to operate in the future so that women's participation rates in the labor force will approach those of men. In 1987, female labor force participation rates for individuals 16 years old and over was 56.0 percent, while male labor force participation rates were 76.2 percent. However, we can expect even higher participation rates by women in the future. Women 20 to 24 years of age were 72.4 percent of the female labor

Table 5.4
Percentage of Females in Selected Occupations 1970, 1980, and 1986

	1970	1980	1986	
			All	Under 35 Years
Percent of employment that is female	38	43	44	45
Managerial and professional	34	41	43	49
Technical, sales and administrative support	59	64	65	66
Service Occupations	60	59	61	58
Precision production, craft and repair	7	8	9	8
Operators, fabricators and laborers	26	27	25	22
Farming, forestry, and fishing	9	15	16	14

Sources: Department of Commerce, Bureau of the Census and
           Department of Labor, BLS.

force, while women 25 to 34 were 71.6 percent. This trend toward increased female labor force participation will increase aggregate GNP and per capita GNP. Assuming that the wage is a measure of productivity, it is evident that output per worker will be reduced. As wages for women approach those of men (discussed below), there will be no decline in productivity associated with increased female labor force participation.

Great changes in the kind of marketplace work by women have taken place since 1970. In 1970, while the female labor force was 38 percent of the total labor force, 34 percent of female workers were in occupations denoted "managerial and professional." (Lines one and two of Table 5.4.) By 1986, the percent of the female labor force was 44 percent of the total labor force and 43 percent of female workers were found in occupations denoted "managerial and professional." It is a striking fact that for those under 35 years the female labor force is 45 percent of the total labor force, while the percent of women in managerial and professional occupations rises to 49 percent!

Thus there is clear evidence that women are leaving occupations

Table 5.5
**Earnings of Females as a Percentage of Earnings of Males (by Age),
1979, 1982, and 1985**

Year	Age of Workers (Years)			
	20-24	25-34	35-44	45-54
1979	76.7	67.5	58.2	57.0
1982	82.4	72.0	61.1	60.0
1985	85.7	75.1	63.2	59.6

Source: Economic Report of the President for 1987, p. 222.

stereotyped as "female" and are moving into occupations stereotyped as "male." For example, in 1970 5 percent of the female labor force were "lawyers and judges"; but by 1986 18 percent were "lawyers and judges." In contrast, 97 percent of the "registered nurses" were female in 1970; by 1986 this fell to 94 percent. This shift in occupations will have an impact on the ratio of female to male wages, to which we turn.

Earnings Patterns

Female workers earn less than male workers. Table 5.5 shows clear-cut patterns. First, female earnings as a percentage of male earnings rose significantly between 1979 and 1985. The highest female earnings as a percentage of male earnings are for those in the 20 to 24 age bracket (85.7 percent). Furthermore, the largest increase in female wages as a percentage of the earnings of males is in the 20 to 24 age bracket. No doubt much of the increase in female earnings relative to male earnings for the youngest age brackets can be accounted for by changes in the occupational distribution. If these trends continue, the gap between male and female workers will, for all practical purposes, disappear in a generation.

A significant amount of the gap between male and female earnings can be accounted for by factors which are nondiscriminatory. Among these factors are (1) hours of work; (2) education; (3) age; (4) union membership; (5) work experience—particularly tenure with one employer. These factors account for about 50 percent of the female-male earnings gap. The remaining unexplained 50 percent of the female-male earnings gap is due to discrimination or to some unmeasured factors. The particular weights to be applied to discrimination and unmeasured factors are a subject of controversy among economists.

Expectations are important in explaining part of the female-male earnings gap:

What and how long women study, what jobs they take, and what occupations they choose depend, in part, upon how long and remunerative they expect their careers to be. The dramatic increases in women's employment were unanticipated. Not surprisingly, many women seriously underestimated how many years they would work in the marketplace. As a result, women on average were less trained for labor market activities than they would have been had they anticipated their future work histories. Today, young women expect to spend a much greater fraction of their adult lives working in the labor market than their mothers did.[5]

We should take note of the fact that there has been the "feminization of poverty" during the last two decades. Women and children are 64 percent of the population, while they represent 77 percent of the poor. Female poverty is related to the rising trend in female-headed households (unwed mothers and divorced mothers). Divorce property settlements are biased against the female—especially when one considers that the female often has less human capital than the male. In addition, men frequently do not fulfill their obligations to support the children. The "feminization of poverty" is probably a transient phenomenon.

To summarize: Women's earnings and productivity are rising at a rapid rate and will have a significant impact on increasing productivity in future decades.

BLACKS IN THE ECONOMY

In 1968, the presidential commission known as the Kerner Commission concluded: "Our nation is moving toward two societies, one black, one white—separate and unequal." Broad aggregate data appear to support this forecast. Between 1970 and 1986, median black *family income* as a percentage of white family income fell from 0.613 to 0.571. Black unemployment rates were roughly twice

Table 5.6
Black-White Income Ratio by Years of Schooling

Years of Schooling	Birth Cohort 1926-1935		Birth Cohort 1936-1945		
	1970	1980	1970	1980	1990[a]
8-11	69.7	75.1	72.8	76.4	80.1
12	70.3	72.0	74.6	79.0	83.5
16+	78.0	79.1	76.7	82.9	89.5

Source: U.S. Census (computer tape) and 1980 Current Population
Survey. Cited by James P. Smith, "Race and Human
Capital," American Economic Review, September 1984,
p. 697.

[a]Projected by author.

white unemployment rates in 1970 and 1986. Though infant mortality rates have fallen for both blacks and whites, black infant mortality was 64 percent higher than that for whites in both 1970 and 1986.

Yet there are positive areas. The workplace is more integrated currently than it was two decades ago. There are many black mayors in major cities. And a considerable black middle class has developed. It is clear that the distribution of black incomes has become more unequal over the past two decades. The growth of the economy has brought prosperity to blacks as well as whites. In fact, the aggregate figures hide data showing some progress for blacks. Thus, between 1970 and 1986 the ratio of median income for black *males* to white males rose slightly from 0.59 in 1970 to 0.60 in 1986. For *male year-round full-time workers* the ratio of median black income to white median income was 0.68 in 1970 and 0.71 in 1986. Thus, some progress is evident for the period 1970 to 1986. Yet these data are still too aggregated—ignoring certain crucial dimensions of black progress.

By disaggregating the data according to years of schooling and by age, an optimistic picture unfolds. (See Table 5.6.) The picture that emerges shows considerable economic progress for blacks.

1. The ratio of black-white income is highest for the younger cohort born between 1936 and 1945. (Those with 16+ schooling

in 1970 are an exception.) This signifies that black-white income ratios will be higher in the future as the older cohorts leave the labor force.

2. The ratio of black-white income is highest for those individuals with the most schooling, except for those with 12 years of schooling in 1980 for the 1926–1935 cohort. Education is the major vehicle for raising black incomes relative to white incomes. We should note that in the past black schools were of a lower quality than white schools.

3. The black-white income ratios increase over time, with 1980 ratios being significantly higher than the 1970 ratios. If we project the 1970–1980 percentage increase to 1990, shown in the last column of Table 5.6, black-white income ratios will have increased dramatically by about 10 percentage points between 1970 and 1990.

To assess prospects for black workers we should examine the underlying economic logic of racial discrimination in the labor market. Can black workers' wages be less than white workers' wages if the productivity of blacks and whites is equal in a competitive economy? The answer is clearly in the negative. If blacks are paid less than whites, firms that do *not* discriminate will hire black workers at the below-average wage, while firms that do discriminate will hire only white workers at the above-average wage. It is difficult to see how firms that discriminate and have higher labor costs could survive in the long run. Consequently, wages of black and white workers would be equalized in equilibrium. In the long run, a discriminating competitive economy is an oxymoron.

Why then has racial discrimination in the labor market diminished at a slower pace than economic theory apparently suggests? Several reasons may be given for the persistence of labor market discrimination.

1. *Markets are not competitive*: If a firm has a strong market position it may be able to "afford" discrimination without jeopardizing its survival. It merely takes less profit, but still survives. In addition, many craft unions have effectively prevented entry of black workers into many occupations. Thus, with blacks forced into lower paying occupations, a lower black-white income ratio results. This suggests that an effective antitrust policy which keeps product and labor markets competitive will go a long way toward ending labor market discrimination. Empirical evidence supports

the conclusion that discrimination is a more serious problem in a noncompetitive setting. This implies that the deregulation of such industries as banking, trucking, airlines, long-distance telephone, and cable TV has been a factor in reducing discrimination.

2. *Expectations of blacks*: Black workers may be less productive because the present situation excessively dominates their expectations. As we emphasize in the section above on women, expectations are extremely important in making educational and occupational choices. If we begin with discrimination, a young black person may have less incentive to become productive because he or she believes discrimination will continue. Believing that discrimination will continue, the black person will have a lower expected rate of return on education than a white person. This is an example of self-fulfilling expectations. Consequently, discrimination feeds upon itself. This implies that the civil rights laws should be effectively enforced so that young blacks can make occupational choices on the perception of a discrimination-free labor market.

3. *Expectations by employers*: Perceptions may exist that, on average, black workers' productivity is poor. Kenneth Arrow has argued that, if employers believe that blacks are less productive than white workers, employers will behave in accordance with their beliefs. This is particularly true where it is costly to determine the productivity of a prospective employee. Following the theory of cognitive dissonance, Arrow argues that

Beliefs and actions should come into some sort of equilibrium; in particular, if individuals act in a discriminatory manner, they will tend to acquire or develop beliefs which justify such actions.[6]

It is difficult to suppose that these beliefs will persist if these perceptions of reality are demonstrated to be in error. However, because employers are probably using adaptive expectations, the correction of error regarding black-worker productivity will take time. Thus black workers who are gaining productivity in the 1980s by accumulating human capital may find that they pay a penalty during a transitional period because they are perceived to be less productive than they actually are. Eventually, however, the error will be corrected.

We shall see progress toward ending discrimination in the labor market if we maintain a competitive economy and raise the expec-

tations of young blacks so that they become more productive—
thereby changing the expectations of employers regarding black
productivity. Empirical evidence as well as theory point to labor
market discrimination diminishing significantly over the next Kondratieff "rise" from 1990 to 2015. Not only will past progress
continue, it may in fact accelerate. This progress has often been
ignored because of the excessive concentration on the short run and
the present condition of the black underclass. We agree with Smith:

During this century, America has undergone an evolutionary process,
spawned in large part in its schools, that permanently altered and improved
the relative economic position of black Americans. Because this process
evolved slowly and because its implications for economic welfare were not
realized until decades after the seeds were planted, the importance and
even the existence of this evolution has been largely ignored or dismissed.[7]

EDUCATIONAL EXPENDITURES AND SCHOLASTIC APTITUDE TEST SCORES

The national spotlight is on education—as it should be. For our
purposes we wish to assess trends in the educational system and to
relate these trends to productivity.

As a nation we are spending more on education. Between 1975
and 1986, expenditure per pupil in daily attendance in 1985 dollars
rose from $2,626 to $3,574. This is a remarkable 2.8 percent annual
increase between 1975 and 1986. Some of this increase may be
related to the fact that attendance fell from 41.4 million in 1975
to 36.6 million in 1986, a decrease of 1.1 percent per year. Some
costs of education, particularly administrative costs, are fixed and
independent of the number of students so that costs per student
will rise as the number of students falls. Furthermore, a smaller
student body may prevent schools from taking advantage of economies of scale.

But the most important reason for the increase in costs per pupil
is related to the higher costs of the teaching staff. Between 1975
and 1986 the number of teachers remained constant, so that the
student-teacher ratio fell; at the same time teachers' salaries increased in real terms by about 2.1 percent annually. Thus it appears
that the public is "buying" more education. These expenditures are
apparently paying off. Table 5.7 shows that Scholastic Aptitude

Table 5.7
Scholastic Aptitude Test Scores 1978 to 1986

Year	Verbal	Mathematics	Total	Number Taking Exam (000)
1978	429	466	895	989
1979	427	467	894	992
1980	424	466	890	992
1981	424	466	890	994
1982	426	467	893	969
1983	425	468	893	963
1984	426	471	897	965
1985	431	475	906	977
1986	431	475	906	1,001
1987	430	476	906	1,080
1988	428	476	904	1,134

Source: College Entrance Board, New York, N.Y.

Test (SAT) scores of high school seniors fell between 1978 and 1981. But after 1981 there is generally a steady increase in SAT scores. This is true for both the verbal and mathematics scores.

It should be noted that the number of students taking the examination varies from year to year, so that the changes in the scores may be related to the varying number taking the examination. One would expect that as more students take the examination, the average score will decrease.[8] However, we should note that between 1983 and 1986 the number taking the examination increased while the scores increased. This makes the increased scores since 1983 all the more impressive. Perhaps it is not coincidental that the highly critical government report *A Nation at Risk* was published in 1983, coinciding with the turnaround in SAT scores. We can expect these improved verbal and mathematical abilities to increase productivity in the future. It is recognized that the achievement levels of American high school students fare poorly when compared with students in other industrialized nations. It is more relevant to emphasize the potential for growth in achievement rather than the level of achievement, since the focus here is on economic growth.

A word should be said about the state of colleges and the American "cultural revolution" of the 1960s. This was a period of great turmoil where older educational goals were devalued and, in general, learning was diminished. Bloom is probably correct when he says

About the sixties it is now fashionable to say that although there were indeed excesses, many good things resulted. But, so far as universities are concerned, I know of nothing positive coming from that period; it was an unmitigated disaster for them. I hear that the good things were "greater openness," "less rigidity," "freedom from authority," etc.—but these have no content and express no view of what is wanted from a university education.[9]

The college student of the sixties often not only lacked a broad liberal arts education, but also often lacked preparation for work. This no doubt contributed to the productivity malaise of the 1970s and the 1980s. Fortunately, students now are more serious and disciplined and the quietus has been put on the American "cultural revolution."

UNION-MANAGEMENT CONFLICT: A BARRIER TO GROWTH?

It may be argued that the above discussion is selective and suffers from the sin of omission. Surely, if one tried it would be possible to enumerate an almost infinite number of structural changes in the economy or the occurrence of exogenous events that would inhibit growth. Many possibilities come to mind: a nuclear holocaust, a great depression, a greenhhouse effect, a breakdown in the international trading system, a population explosion, antigrowth public policy, union-management strife. If we deal with *probabilities* which are significantly different from zero, the list is severely reduced. All bets are off if there is a nuclear holocaust. The probability of a great depression occurring again is practically zero—thanks to J. M. Keynes. We shall deal with the probabilities of a breakdown in the international trading system, a population explosion, and antigrowth policies in future chapters. Let us turn to the problem of union-management conflict serving as a possible damper on growth.

Table 5.8
Payoff to Union Workers and Management for Different Strategies

		Union Strategy	
		Adversial	Cooperate
Management	Adversial	10 \10	15 \5
Strategy	Cooperate	5 \15	20 \20

Various union policies (e.g., jurisdictional disputes, make-work rules, excessively long apprenticeship periods, exclusion of minorities) as well as management policies (e.g., union-busting, speed-up) have probably reduced the rate of economic growth in the past. However, union-management relations in the last decade have probably moved from adversarial to cooperative. The reason this is happening is that both management and unions have learned that payoffs are highest when they cooperate. Let us explain this shift in union-management relations by a specific illustration.

Suppose you have a group of unionized skilled workers dealing with management. And suppose consideration is given to installing a new technology in the workplace. Table 5.8 shows the strategies and payoffs available to the union and management. Management's payoffs are expressed as a rate of return on net worth and are shown in the southwest part of each cell; the union workers' payoff, expressed as a rate of return on their human capital, is shown in the northeast part of each cell.

If management is *adversarial*, it promises not to pink slip workers when the new technology is in place, but in fact management does pink slip workers. If management is *cooperative*, it keeps its promise not to pink slip workers when the new technology is in place.

If the union is *adversarial*, it promises not to oppose the new technology, but in fact it does oppose installation of the new technology by engaging in a slowdown. If the union is *cooperative*, it keeps its promise not to oppose the new technology.

It is evident that the best of all possible worlds would be one where both parties cooperated and kept their promises, thereby receiving a 20 percent return. If both parties were adversarial, the return would be cut in half to 10 percent. The worst of all possible worlds for the union would be one where they cooperated, but management was adversarial; the worst of all possible worlds for management would be where they cooperated, but the union was adversarial.

Given these payoffs, if both the union and management have an adversarial policy they at least guarantee that their minimum return will be no lower than 10 percent. If one party was cooperative and the other party was adversarial, the return to the cooperating party would go to 5 percent. If the parties did not trust one another—a situation that was probably not uncommon prior to the 1980s—then each would choose an adversarial strategy ending with a payoff of 10 percent. But clearly this involves a great missed opportunity associated with a 20 percent return *if both* parties cooperate.

One possible way to ensure that both parties will cooperate is to find a third party who can somehow convince each party that the other party will cooperate. However, it is often difficult to find an effective disinterested third party. A more common approach is to become cooperative on the basis of experience. In a market-oriented economy, the more powerful party is usually management. It has the power over time to convince the union to cooperate because it can afford to take the risk of temporary losses occurring when it initiates cooperation. If management initiates cooperation and continues to cooperate and the union reciprocates, both parties have a maximum return of 20 percent. If the union insists on remaining adversarial, management then reciprocates by also being adversarial, reducing the union workers' return to 10 percent. Thus the union is faced with the choice of taking a 15 percent return in the short run, but ending up with a 10 percent return in the long run, or getting a 20 percent return over the long run because it has learned by experience to trust management. Union-management relations, like life, are reciprocal.

The 1980s witnessed an increasingly union-management co-operative spirit. This is illustrated by the various profit-sharing agreements reached in the automobile industry. It seems highly probable that this cooperative spirit will continue into the future. We may conclude that union-management conflict will not be a barrier to higher growth rates. In fact, it may make a positive contribution to the goal of a higher rate of economic growth.

SUMMARY

Many favorable structural changes will occur in the next few decades to increase the rate of economic growth in the United States. The growth rate of the service sector will tend to diminish the severity of the business cycle. Perhaps the long period of growth from 1983 to 1989 is a harbinger of things to come. Furthermore, with fewer young workers and more full-time, year-round female workers, the effective labor force will increase. Also the better educated labor force will increase the effective labor force. Finally, it is expected that diminished discrimination against female and black workers will have a positive impact on the rate of economic growth. These changes signify that the effective labor force will grow at a minimum twice as fast as population growth, thereby increasing economic growth.[10]

NOTES

1. Evsey Domar, *Essays in the Theory of Economic Growth* (Oxford University Press, Oxford, 1957), p. 14.

2. Lawrence R. Klein and Joel Popkin, "An Econometric Analysis of Postwar Relationship between Inventory Fluctuations and Changes in Aggregate Economic Activity," in *Inventory Fluctuations and Economic Stabilization*, Joint Economic Committee, 87th Congress, 1st Session, 1961, part 3, p. 75. For a theoretical approach germane to this discussion see Lloyd A. Metzler, "The Nature and Stability of Inventory Cycles," *Review of Economics and Statistics* 23 (June 1941), pp. 113–29. Ray Fair found inventory shocks significant. ("Sources of Economic Fluctuations in the United States," *Quarterly Journal of Economics* (May 1988)).

3. The "payback" criterion for investment emphasizing immediate payoffs has the potential for producing disaster. For example, suppose one invests $100 with cash flows of $50 in the first year, $50 in the second year, and zero in the third year. This has a payback of two years, that is, the initial investment will be recovered in two years. Compare this with a second investment which also involves an initial investment of $100, but with cash flows of zero, zero, and $150 over three years, respectively. This investment has a payback of 2.6. It appears that the first investment is superior since it has a lower payback period. However, it is clear that at, say, a cost of funds of 10 percent, the first investment with a net present value of -$13.3 should be rejected and the second investment with a net present value of $2.78 should be accepted. The myopic payback investment

criterion, emphasizing inordinately the short run will become less significant, with the result that investment errors will also diminish.

4. Darby, "U.S. Productivity Slowdown," p. 317.

5. *Economic Report of the President, 1987*, pp. 215–16.

6. Kenneth J. Arrow, "The Theory of Discrimination," in Orley Ashenfelter and Arthur Rees (eds.), *Discrimination in Labor Markets* (Princeton University Press, 1974), p. 26. Also see E. S. Phelps, "The Statistical Theory of Racism and Sexism." *American Economic Review*, September 1972.

7. James P. Smith, "Race and Human Capital," *American Economic Review*, September 1984, p. 697.

8. We found this to be true. Using state data in 1988, the coefficient of correlation between the mathematics score and the percentage of graduate students in the state taking the SAT examination was −0.861.

9. Alan Bloom, *The Closing of the American Mind* (Simon & Schuster, New York, 1987), p. 320.

10. Summarizing the conclusions of the last few chapters quantitatively, suppose the aggregate production function reads: $Y = AK^{.3}N^{.7}$, where Y, K, and N are GNP, the services of the capital stock and the services of the labor force, respectively. An increase in the constant, A, represents an increase in productivity because of such factors as technological advance, demographic changes, and diminished discrimination. Letting a dot over the variable represent "percentage change," the growth of GNP per worker, $\dot{Y} - \dot{N}$, equals $\dot{A}/.7$. It is argued here that on average $\dot{A}$ will *at least* equal 1.75 to give a growth rate of GNP per worker averaging *at least* 2.5 percent over the next 25 years or so. Per worker GNP growth rates are very closely related to per captita GNP growth rates. Note that we are assuming that the capital-output ratio remains constant.

6

The International Dimension

It is the maxim of every prudent master of a family never to attempt to make at home what it will cost him more to make than to buy. ...What is prudence in the conduct of every private family, can scarce be folly in that of a great kingdom.[1]

Increased trade (in the post-World War II period) has contributed substantially to the increase in productivity, both because countries have been able to specialize more on the things they do best and because the pressure of competition has been increased.[2]

The international economic system is an intricate and delicate web of interlocking strands. Great opportunities exist for advancing economic development in the comity of nations as the world moves closer and closer to the free movement of goods, people, and ideas.

Previous chapters focused on the United States and the causes that justify the forecast of a significantly higher per capita income growth rate over the next 25 years or so. In this chapter it will be emphasized that the United States is not an island. What happens in the United States often has a profound effect elsewhere. And, in this rapidly changing universe, events elsewhere have an impact on the United States. The entity called "the U.S. economy" (or, for that matter "the French economy") is slowly but inevitably passing from the scene and the world economy is emerging.

In the emerging world economy, free trade will be applied more extensively. Free trade, as we will show, will produce significant gains because of a better allocation of international resources and because of improvements in productivity associated with the international transfer of technology. The history of the past century dramatically illustrates that international events transcend political boundaries. If there is growth, this leaves room for profound optimism.

PROSPECTS FOR EXPANSION OF FREE TRADE

In Chapter 5 it was stressed that economic growth can take place because of an improved allocation of resources in the absence of technological advance. The focus in that chapter was on domestic changes in the structure of the U.S. economy. Here we shall place emphasis on structural changes in the international economy that are expected to characterize the economy for the next few decades.

International trade is an engine of growth. Growth is based on the gains associated with trade consistent with the operation of the principle of comparative advantage. International trade and investment produce dynamic gains from trade, which also stimulates growth. These dynamic forces will be discussed below.

Prior to the development of classical economics, it was commonly believed by the so-called mercantilists as well as most public officials that one nation's gain was another nation's loss. The mercantilist view held sway between 1500 and 1750. The mercantilists believed that the world output was more or less fixed, so that *both* parties to a transaction could not gain simultaneously. With this type of thought dominating, it is little wonder that the mercantilist period was characterized by frequent commercial wars—a situation Eli Hecksher termed the "tragedy of mercantilism." War was thought to be a constant-sum game—what the winner in war gained, the loser lost.[3]

Beginning with Adam Smith and refined by David Ricardo, the mercantilist's "common sense" was challenged. More positively, these economists convinced public officials that free trade was the best policy, because all nations can gain from trade. Thus a policy of free trade became a major source of economic growth in the nineteenth century. Free trade operates as if there is a "free lunch" because of an improved allocation of resources. (The reader who

Table 6.1
Hypothetical Output per Unit of Input of Fruit and Oil in the United States and Canada

	United States	Canada
Fruit	12	4
Oil	6	4
Ratio of price of fruit to price of oil	0.5	1.0

is convinced that free trade maximizes output may skip the discussion of this section without a loss of continuity.)

The essential logic of the theory of comparative advantage can be spelled out where there are only two countries and two commodities. Table 6.1 shows the hypothetical output per unit of input of fruits and oil in the United States and Canada. These outputs vary because of different endowment of resources or because of different levels of technology in the two countries.

Before trade is established between Canada and the United States, the price of fruit is one-half the price of oil in the United States. That is, in the United States the cost of oil is twice as high as the cost of fruit, since productivity of oil output per unit of input is one-half that of fruit. In Canada the price of a unit of fruit will equal the price of a unit of oil.

When trade is established between Canada and the United States, both nations can gain because the price structures are different in the two countries. Aside from differences in consumer tastes, if the price structures were identical there would be no opportunity to gain from trade. The United States has a *comparative* advantage in the production of fruit, and it will produce and export fruit to Canada, and it will stop producing oil, requiring it to import oil from Canada. Note that this is true even though the United States has an *absolute* advantage in the production of oil, being able to produce more oil per unit of input than Canada. A baseball parallel would be helpful here. Suppose Pete Rose is a better than average first baseman and is also considered a genius as manager of the team. It would be rational for Pete to stop playing first base and devote all his time to managing the team. The opportunity cost of playing first base (giving up time for management) exceeds the benefits from playing first base.

With the establishment of trade, one unit of fruit exported to Canada will buy one unit of oil in Canada, a net gain for the United States over the situation that existed before trade was established. Similarly, Canada has a comparative advantage (or, least comparative disadvantage) in the production of oil. Therefore, Canada will produce oil for export to the United States and import fruit from the United States. In the process Canada will have a net gain because a unit of its oil will now buy two units of fruit in the United States. To repeat, international trade operates as if there is a "free lunch."

As trade takes place in this newly established Canadian-American common market, there must be an equalization of the price of each good in equilibrium. This also means that a common price ratio will be established in equilibrium somewhere between 0.5, the United States pretrade ratio of prices, and 1.0, the Canadian pretrade ratio of prices. If the equilibrium price ratio were one-half (i.e., the price of fruit is one-half the price of oil), all the gain would accrue to Canada and the United States would experience no gain. This is evident since the price of fruit has fallen relative to the price of oil for Canadians; but from the vantage point of the United States, there has been no change in the price of oil relative to the price of fruit. At the other extreme, if the price ratio in equilibrium were equal to one, all the gain from trade would accrue to the United States; Canada would experience no gain.

If the equilibrium price ratio after trade is established lies somewhere between 0.5 and 1.0, *both* nations gain from trade. For example, if a price ratio of 0.7 is established, one unit of Canadian oil can buy 1.4 (i.e., 1/0.7) units of fruit from the United States—an improvement over the pretrade situation when one unit of oil bought only one unit of fruit. Similarly, one unit of U.S. fruit can now buy 0.7 units of oil—an improvement for the United States over the pretrade situation when one unit of fruit purchased only one-half unit of oil. Trade improves economic welfare by lowering the price of the good in which the nation does *not* have a comparative advantage.

On logical grounds the price ratio of the larger economy (i.e., the United States with the larger GNP) would tend to prevail. It follows that, while both nations gain from trade, the greatest gain accrues to the smaller economy (i.e., Canada with the smaller GNP). For example, if the ratio of the fruit price to the oil price is 0.55—closer to the pretrade U.S. price ratio than to the pretrade Canadian price ratio—both nations would gain, but the Canadians would gain more than the Americans. Put differently, the Canadian terms of trade, that is, the price of exports divided by the price of imports, improve. The price of oil over the price of fruit is now 1.82, equal to 1/0.55. We shall return to the problem of the terms of trade below.

The above illustration is simplified. However, complications, to which we turn, do not change the basic conclusion that a movement from restricted to free trade expands GNP and is a cause of economic growth. The first complication refers to the assumption that all firms are in competition, so that in the long run price will just cover cost. However, if, say, the United States had a monopoly in fruit, they could charge a price which exceeds costs and earn monopoly profits at the expense of the Canadians. Given the openness of the modern economy, the assumption of competition is reasonable.

Second, we have assumed that transport costs and other barriers to trade are absent. If these costs are important, the price of fruit, for example, will be higher in Canada than in the United States. Cost-reducing innovations in transportation have been a handmaiden to the expansion of world commerce, tending to equalize prices throughout the world.

Third, we have assumed that the average costs per unit are constant as output varies; for example, a doubling of fruit output will not change the average cost per unit of fruit. If there are diminishing returns in the production of fruit, the average cost of production for fruit will rise, increasing its price. If the price of American fruit increases sufficiently, it would be rational at some point for the Canadians to supplement the American fruit supply. Pursuing this illustration further, it is also possible for the average cost per unit to be lower as the output of fruit expands because of economies of scale. In this case, the price of fruit will decrease. An opening up of trade can be a boon to a small country such as Taiwan or Yugoslavia with a small domestic market. An opening up of trade expands the size of the market and permits the small country to take advantage of economies of scale.

Not only will product prices tend to be equalized internationally, but factor prices (i.e, wages, interest rates) will also tend to be equalized. For example, a country with a relative abundance of labor will tend to produce goods which are labor-intensive. The increase in demand for these labor-intensive goods resulting from the opening up of trade will tend to increase the derived demand for labor. This will increase wage rates, bringing them closer to those in other nations. In other nations, where labor is relatively scarce, exports will tend to be capital-intensive so that the derived demand for labor decreases and wages fall. The net result will be an equalization of wage rates internationally.[4] Wage rate equalization could be achieved if labor migrated internationally, with labor moving away from the low-wage areas and moving toward the high-wage areas. Wages would increase in the nation losing workers and fall in the nation gaining workers. Thus population movements are a partial substitute for movement of goods. For example, Mexican workers' economic lot can be improved by increasing Mexico's export of goods or Mexico can "export" workers to the United States.

Generally, we tend to overestimate the importance of blue-collar wage costs. Blue-collar wage costs are becoming a minor factor in the location decision, because they are a declining percentage of total cost. Blue-collar costs in the United States are about 18 percent of total costs and falling. Suppose it is required that offshore total costs must be at least 6 percent lower at an offshore location than at a U.S. location to offset the additional transport costs from offshore locations. Also assume that the wage cost is 18 percent of total cost in the United States. Under these conditions, it would take a minimum of a 33 percent lower blue-collar wage offshore compared to the blue-collar wage in the United States to induce firms to locate offshore. Because of the relative decline in blue-collar wage costs and the relative increase in transport costs, more and more multinational firms are tending to locate where the market is.

Fourth, the model of comparative advantage assumes that there is full employment of all resources. In fact, there may be a surplus of natural resources or unemployed labor—a situation not uncommon in many low-income, developing countries. This involves a long-run disequilibrium. As natural resources are exploited, a wave of growth will occur. The history of Canada illustrates this case.

Canadian development over three centuries was unleashed by the export of such staples as fish, furs, grain, pulp and paper, and petroleum.[5] The early history of the United States is not dissimilar from that of the Canadian experience. W. Arthur Lewis[6] discussed growth where there are practically unlimited labor supplies. Lewis believed that the marginal product of labor might be zero in the subsistence sector. Thus, a significant amount of labor could be removed from the subsistence sector with no loss of output. This labor could be employed in the export sector at a zero opportunity cost.

Fifth, the expansion of trade often produces dynamic gains which result in increased productivity. As trade expands, international investment expands. And often international investment is the vehicle for bringing forth new ideas and technological advance. When a multinational firm establishes a modern plant in a low-income nation there frequently are significant increases in productivity associated with "learning by doing." The very presence of a mass-production steel or automobile industry helps to instill more efficient work habits. Unskilled workers perform better on production which is dominated by the speed of the machine than on production which is dominated by the speed of the worker. These dynamic linkages between the export sector and the domestic sectors not only increase productivity but may significantly increase employment. In addition, the expansion of trade and the increased international contacts will produce "demonstration effects," with a greater variety of consumer goods being demanded.

These dynamic gains from trade are particularly important for small countries such as South Korea and Yugoslavia. The empirical evidence for the significant link between growth and international trade is strong. For small countries there is a positive correlation between the level and rate of economic development and the export-GNP ratio.

The above example assumes that productivity increases are the same in fruit and oil, so that the price structure remains unchanged. If productivity increased at a greater rate in the oil sector in Canada, oil prices would fall relative to fruit prices. This may reduce the terms of trade for Canada. However, this does not necessarily reduce Canada's gain from trade, since more oil can be sold at the lower prices.

The Canadian Connection

The above discussion may be old hat for readers who have had a course in elementary economics. But it is intended to have the reader take the theory of comparative advantage seriously. Let us go from the hypothetical to the not-so-hypothetical case of Canadian-American trade to illustrate that the benefits from free trade are not some Panglossian nonsense. The symbiotic nature of Canadian-American trade is clear, when we realize that Canada is the United States's largest trading partner, having 18.9 percent of U.S. trade in 1987. The United States had 71.1 percent of Canadian trade in 1987.

Many efforts have been made to create freer trade between Canada and the United States. In the 1840s, Canada initiated negotiations for free trade in response to England's unilateral move toward free trade. In 1854, the United States and Canada signed a treaty which covered trade in natural products and expanded both nations' fishing rights. Tariff levels have varied. In the 1850s, the average U.S. tariff was 27 percent, while the Canadian tariffs averaged 16 percent. Tariff rates reached new highs in 1930, when U.S. tariffs were increased to an average of 59 percent and Canadian tariffs were 24 percent. Currently, the U.S. tariff averages about 4 percent and the Canadian tariff is 7 percent. Three-fourths of U.S.-Canadian trade is not subject to tariffs. In 1987, a free trade agreement was signed by Prime Minister Mulroney and President Reagan. The main provision of the agreement is for the elimination of all tariffs beginning January 1, 1989. Depending on the product, bilateral tariffs will be eliminated immediately or over a period of 5 or 10 years. In addition, many nontariff barriers will be eased. For example, the two countries have agreed to recognize each other's system for laboratory accreditation. This will avoid duplication and should increase the rate at which new pharmaceutical products are brought to the market. The agreement will be monitored by a Canadian-U.S. Trade Commission to implement the treaty.

It has been estimated that the gain to the United States runs between $1.1 and $2.9 billion annually.[7] The Canadian gain is about the same. Since Canadian GNP is much smaller than the American GNP, the Canadian gain as a percentage of GNP is much greater than that of the United States. Put another way, these estimates indicate that the growth rate for the United States will be increased by about 0.04 percent (i.e., $2 billion gain—the mid-point between $1.1 and $2.9 billion—divided by a GNP of $5,000 billion). For example, without the agreement the GNP growth rate might be 3.00 percent; with the agreement the GNP growth rate would be 3.04 percent. The increase in the Canadian GNP growth rate will be greater since its GNP is smaller than that of the United States.

These estimates of gain are probably too conservative. They do not take account of the gains resulting from increased economies of scale because of an expanded market size. Nor do they take account of the dynamic gains discussed above.

This increase in the growth rate also appears small because it is applied to only 18.9 percent of U.S. trade. If such gains could be achieved between the United States and all its trading partners by freeing world trade, the growth rate would increase by about 0.26 percent. It should be noted that the potential gains from an agreement between the United States and its non-Canadian trading partners are greater than the gains from the Canadian-American agreement. This results because barriers to trade are greater between the United States and its non-Canadian trading partners than are the barriers to trade between the United States and Canada. Furthermore, the differences in price structures between the United States and its non-Canadian trading partners are greater than the differences between the United States and Canada. The greater the differences in price structures, the greater the opportunity for gains from trade. This implies that the gains from trade are very significant for trade between the United States and developing countries. The increase in growth rates in the rest of the world would be even greater since GNPs are smaller. In any event, an increase of 0.26 percent *and higher* in the growth rate is clearly significant.

The Canadian-American agreement is an interesting illustration of the "prisoner's dilemma" problem. This analysis closely parallels the analysis of labor-management conflict in Chapter 5. Let us concentrate on Table 6.2. The table shows that the United States and Canada, acting independently, have two choices: to protect trade or to follow a policy of free trade. The numbers in the table represent the ranking of the payoffs with four being the highest. The number in the southwest part of the cell is the payoff for the United States and the number in the northeast part is the payoff

Table 6.2
Payoff to Canada and the United States for Different Strategies

		Canadian Strategy	
		Protection	Free Trade
U.S. Strategy	Protection	2\2	3\1
	Free Trade	1\3	4\4

for Canada. For example, if both nations choose a policy of protection, each would receive a payoff of two.

Notice that the payoff is highest if both nations choose free trade since international trade increases the income of both nations. If the United States chooses free trade it would get a payoff of four *if* Canada also chooses free trade. But *if* Canada chooses a policy of protection, the United States' payoff will be one. In the face of the uncertainty regarding Canadian choices, it may be rational for the United States to minimize its losses by choosing a policy of protection. That is, if the United States chooses protection, the lowest payoff it can get is two; but if it chooses free trade, the lowest payoff is one. Therefore a policy of protection is preferred. And, of course, the Canadians are in the same position as the United States and may find it best to choose a policy of protection. It is evident that we can avoid this dilemma if international institutions are so designed that each nation follows a policy of free trade because they are assured that other nations will also follow free trade. This game theory framework can help us understand tariff making in the past and help us forecast the future. In 1930 the United States took the initiative by choosing protection with the passage of the Smoot-Hawley Tariff Act. Tariffs were increased to the highest level in American history, averaging 59 percent by 1932. As would be expected, this led other nations to choose a reciprocal policy of protection. This general level of protection throughout the world severely reduced the volume of international trade and intensified the Great Depression. The Smoot-Hawley Tariff Act was a terrible mistake. Fortunately, the United States appears to have learned something from this mistake.

In 1934, with the passage of the Trade Agreements Act, the United States learned how to play the game so that all nations might gain from trade. This act gave the president power to negotiate reciprocal tariff reductions of as much as 50 percent with other nations. This insulated the president from powerful interests who sought higher tariffs through congressional action. Note that in this game there is, practically speaking, an infinite number of plays as we go through time. With the Trade Agreements Act, the United States chose free trade. This created confidence in our trading partners to also play free trade. The policy of choosing free trade has its risks, since if the Canadians choose a policy of protection they will impose losses on the United States. We would expect the United States, generally being the more powerful nation, to take these risks since they can bear the possible losses with less pain than other nations. The Trade Agreements Act has been renewed eleven times. By 1947 tariffs were 50 percent below the 1934 level.

The United States took the initiative to free Canadian-American trade with the passage of the Trade Agreement Act of 1979. This act instructed the president to pursue trade agreements with Canada and Mexico. The Canadians reciprocated in 1985 when a Canadian Royal Commission concluded that it was in Canada's best interest to negotiate mutual tariff reduction in the United States.

In November 1987, the United States and Mexico concluded an agreement to consult over common trade and investment issues. This may lead to a further freeing of trade between Mexico and the United States. Again the United States, the stronger nation, is taking risks in a good cause. Thus there is a good probability that we shall see a vast and prosperous free trade area in North America.

The movement away from protection depends crucially on how tariff-making institutions are structured. If each tariff takes a separate bill in Congress, as in the United States prior to the 1930s, then we can be sure of ending up with a high level of protection, with all its negative consequences. But if we examine tariffs globally, as we have in the Trade Agreement Act of 1933 and the Canadian-American agreement of 1987, we may mutually secure the benefits of free trade.

This is not to deny that there are industries and workers who will be hurt by freer trade in the short run (e.g., the fruit growers in Canada in the illustration above). However, since the net benefits are greater with free trade than with protection it should be possible (as in the Trade Expansion Act of 1962) to extend some aid to the "losers" in the form of low-cost loans to firms and extended unemployment compensation to workers and worker retraining. This would not only lessen the loss to the "losers," it would also weaken the political opposition to free trade.

The GATT Connection

World trade has flowered since World War II. Between 1952 and 1987, world output grew at a 4.5 percent annual rate, while the volume of international trade increased at a 6.5 percent annual rate. This improved allocation of world resources has been a major source of the world's rising standard of living. Important as a stimulus to opening up trade has been the establishment of the General Agreement on Tariffs and Trade (GATT) immediately after World War II.

The GATT's aim is to reduce barriers to trade among its 95 signatory governments. There is a general recognition that mutually lowered tariffs and the minimization of barriers to trade would benefit all nations. Furthermore, it is stressed that tariff concessions should be made by consultation, and that once they are made they cannot be rescinded. The industrialized nations have accepted a principle of the double standard. While industrialized nations will lower tariffs and make trade freer, lower income nations are allowed to utilize barriers to trade to permit them to catch up with the industrialized nations.

The use of a double standard had widespread support as long as the industrialized nations were growing at a healthy rate. But with the beginning of the Kondratieff "decline" starting around 1970 and the onset of stagflation and apparent deindustrialization, many industrialized nations have been increasingly reluctant to accept the double standard.

Countries that have blocked industrialized nations' exports have and will continue to face retaliation. The Japanese in particular have restricted entry of American exports in the construction, financial services, and agricultural sectors—sectors where the United States has a comparative advantage. One can expect the increased pressure in the form of possible retaliation to compel the Japanese to open their markets. The growing world economy in the 1990s will make the transition to free trade easier for the Japanese, as well as for other nations following a mercantilist-type policy.

Since World War II there have been eight GATT negotiating rounds. The latest is the Uruguay Round, which started in September 1986 and is expected to last into the 1990s. The GATT's authority will probably be expanded to cover intellectual property rights, services, investment, and agriculture—areas which were excluded from the original GATT agreement. Intellectual property rights in the form of trademarks, copyrights, and patents have been infringed on a large scale. It has been estimated that lost sales from infringement by firms holding the patent are large, though difficult to estimate. Infringement reduces the rate of return on new ideas. To the extent that infringement can be reduced, the incentive for producing new ideas will be enhanced.

In the Uruguay Round there will be efforts made to free investment flows from such restrictions as domestic content requirements and exchange controls. As we emphasized above, trade and investment go hand in hand.

Agriculture is heavily subsidized in the industrialized world. Federal government outlays in the United States were $26 billion in 1986. The Common Market countries impose costs on taxpayers and consumers amounting to about $60 billion annually. Japanese support in the rice market keeps rice prices almost five times higher than the world price. The United States has proposed that all subsidies to agriculture be eliminated in 10 years, and that all barriers to agricultural imports be eliminated. In a world of free trade in agricultural products, the United States would stop producing sugar, the Common Market would stop producing wheat, and Japan would stop producing rice. The net result would be an increase in economic growth and improved welfare throughout the world.

Cries for protection of domestic industries will continue, and in some cases will succeed. Many Americans, particularly aspiring politicians, lament the fact that America is "losing control of its destiny." Coupled with this is the belief that American firms cannot compete in international markets. Much of this pessimistic view is rooted in the failure of expectations bred during the 1950s when exports of American firms were prized. It is puzzling why Americans are so surprised that other nations, devastated by World War II, have been revitalized, giving the U.S. firms competition in the world market.

And to the extent that the American economy is increasingly open to foreign trade, it loses some control over its destiny. American public policy—particularly monetary and fiscal policy—becomes less important and the international market becomes more dominant. This is one of the "costs" of free trade. In any event, with the expected higher growth rates beginning in the 1990s, these cries for protection will be muted. If economic growth is above average and, say, the United States suffers a loss of its international market share, it does not necessarily follow that American exports absolutely decline. Here we have a benign circle: Free trade causes economic growth and economic growth causes free trade. The relative prosperity of England in the 1840s served as a catalyst for reducing tariffs; and the relative prosperity in the United States in the 1950s and 1960s was a positive force for the reduction of trade barriers.

DISSENTING VIEWS

"Backwash" Argument

The Swedish economist Gunnar Myrdal has argued that the linkages from the export sector to the domestic sectors are often weak. The "backwash" argument does not deny that trade along the lines of comparative advantage discussed above will lead to mutual benefits. However, it is claimed that the manufacturing sector tends to be isolated from the other sectors in a less developed country so that little economic growth occurs. Thus the less developed country is locked into producing agricultural and mining output. In contrast, the industrialization in the higher income nations tends to be self-perpetuating.

In the optimal situation, the dynamic forces resulting from increased investment and exports would work to create a strong stimulus to increasing productivity and employment. This would increase incomes which would then be spent on domestic consumer goods, replacing imports. Here the linkage between trade and growth is significant.

However, another scenario is possible. The dynamic linkage between the export sector may be weak. The development of the tea industry in Ceylon (now Sri Lanka) is illustrative. The tea was transported in British ships, the managers were British, and the capital goods came from Britain. The managers even imported British consumer goods. And profits from the tea industry were repatriated back to Britain. Other examples of weak dynamic linkages are the exploitation of copper in Chile and tin in Malaysia. Frequently local employment effects are minimal because production processes are capital-intensive, in spite of a relative abundance of labor.

This picture of a "dual" economy, with a foreign-dominated small modern enclave and a large agrarian domestic economy, is caused by the problem of underdevelopment and not by international trade. International trade and investment is a necessary but not a sufficient condition for growth and development for nations with a small resource base. International trade and investment, combined with the capacity to respond to the export sector, will produce growth and development. This capacity to respond in turn will depend on such factors as the rate of literacy, tax policies, and political stability.

"Terms of Trade" Argument

The terms of trade is defined as the ratio of export to import prices. Raul Prebisch and Hans Singer have concluded that the less developed countries, producers of primary products, suffer because the terms of trade fall as international trade takes place. In other words, for a typical less developed country more and more exports are required to buy the same quantity of imports. In high-income countries, manufactured goods productivity increases are passed on to workers in the form of higher wages—not lower prices. In contrast, productivity increases in less developed countries are reflected in lower prices. These falling export prices relative to import prices are considered to be unfavorable and rising export prices relative to import prices are considered to be favorable. It follows that the gain from international trade accrues mainly to the high-income industrialized nations.

It is fallacious to use the terms of trade as an index of the gains from trade when there are significant differences in productivity increases in different industries. As we discussed above, if there is an above-average increase in productivity in the export sector, one would expect a decline in the terms of trade. Increased productivity lowers price and results in a larger volume of exports to be sold. If the percentage increase in the volume of exports exceeds the percentage decrease in price, export revenue will increase. In Japan between 1960 and 1980 the terms of trade fell from 150 to 77, with 1975 equal to 100. For Japan, the lower export prices supported by above-average productivity increases was a key to its success. This same pattern has been observed in South Korea and Taiwan over the past two decades.

The terms of trade for the less-developed countries can fall for other reasons than changes in productivity. Primary product prices may fall relatively because of low income elasticities or because labor supplies are more elastic in the less developed countries than in the industrialized countries. Also, prices may be more rigid downward in the industrialized countries compared with the less developed countries. On the other hand, as the classical writers emphasized, diminishing returns in the less developed countries producing primary products would be more significant than in the industrialized countries. This would tend to increase the terms of trade for the less developed countries.

A mountain of academic papers have been spawned to determine the actual trend in the terms of trade. A hung jury has resulted, with some papers showing a rising trend, some a falling trend, and some no trend. This empirical evidence is beside the point, because the theoretical basis is poor for judging whether the less developed countries gain more or less than the industrialized countries.

Parallel arguments, which are equally ridiculous, are perpetrated by the farm lobby in the United States. The argument goes that technological advance and weak demand for agricultural output lower the price farmers receive for their products relative to the prices farmers pay. Therefore, it is argued, the government must intervene to make sure the terms of trade for the farmer do not decline. An examination of data shows that this argument holds little water. Between 1977 and 1987 the prices farmers received increased by 27 percent, while the prices farmers paid increased by 62 percent. The farmers are clearly worse off *if* no other changes took place. But other changes did take place. Output per hour in the business sector grew at 10.5 percent between 1977 and 1987, while farm productivity grew at 27 percent. In addition, the number

Table 6.3
Growth Rates of Per Capita Gross National Product, 1870 to 1964
(percent)

Country	Growth Rate
United States	1.9
Japan	2.5[a]
Germany	1.7
United Kingdom	1.3
France	1.5
Italy	1.4
Canada	1.7
Sweden	2.1[a]

Source: Long-Term Economic Growth, 1860-1965, U.S.
Department of Commerce, October 1966, p. 101.

[a]From 1870 to 1981, from Robert J. Gordon, Macroeconomics,
3d ed., Little Brown, p. 571.

of farmers decreased by 16 percent over this decade, so that net profits for the farmers still in business did not decrease. In spite of these facts, super subsidies persist. In this Alice in Wonderland world, the U.S. government pours over $25 billion annually into the farm economy to prosperous farmers to maintain "parity" in the agricultural terms of trade. The above-average growth of productivity in agriculture is the major cause for the decline in agricultural terms of trade. The terms of trade argument is as fallacious in domestic agriculture as it is in international trade.[8]

GETTING ON THE GROWTH BANDWAGON: THE INDUSTRIALIZED NATIONS

Never before in the history of mankind have we witnessed economic progress like that of the last century in the industrialized nations. Table 6.3 shows that growth rates of per capita GNP for eight nations from 1870 to 1964 have averaged 1.8 percent annually. The growth rates are strikingly similar, except for Japan and Sweden. A major reason for the higher growth rates for these two countries is that they start from a low base. Per capita GNP in 1870 in Japan and Sweden was $596 and $1,044, respectively. In contrast, per capita GNP in 1870 in the United Kingdom and the United States was $2,000 and $1,565, respectively.

Table 6.4 shows growth rates of aggregate GNP for various nations since the 1960s. After the 1960s, growth rates generally decline. This is characteristic of the declining phase of the Kondratieff cycle referred to earlier. Recall that Maddison (in Table 3.3) produces data showing that growth rates vary cyclically over the long cycle from 1870 to 1973. Note that growth rates range between 2.5 and 5.0 percent with the following exceptions:

1. Growth rates for Japan average in double digits between 1961 and 1970.

2. Chinese growth rates are very high and rising, particularly in the 1980s.

3. Developing economies experience growth rates which exceed those of OECD nations from 1961 to 1980. However, when we move from aggregate GNP to per capita GNP growth rates it may not be true that developing economy growth rates are higher than those of the OECD nations because of differential population growth rates.

4. Excluding China, Communist nations, like the OECD nations, show a general pattern of declining GNP growth rates. This suggests that the Kondratieff cycle is present in both the market-oriented capitalistic and the centrally planned socialistic nations.

There is clear evidence of a convergence of growth rates of GNP per capita over the last century. Baumol has provided evidence that, for 16 industrialized nations, per capita GNP has converged, with the deviation from the mean per capita income steadily falling. Baumol emphasizes that there are significant spillover effects of innovation, linking the leading nation in terms of per capita GNP to other nations:

. . . the spillovers from the leader economies to followers are large—at least among the group of industrial nations. If country A's extraordinary investment level and superior record of innovation enhances its own productivity, it will almost automatically do the same in the long run for industrialized country B, though perhaps to a somewhat more limited

Table 6.4
Growth Rate in Real Gross National Product, 1961 to 1987

Area and Country	1961-65 annual average	1966-70 annual average	1971-75 annual average	1976-80 annual average	1981	1982	1983	1984	1985	1986	1987[a]
OECD countries[b]	5.3	4.6	3.0	3.3	2.1	-0.2	2.7	4.7	3.2	2.7	2.8
United States	4.6	3.0	2.2	3.4	1.9	-2.5	3.6	6.8	3.0	2.9	2.9
Canada	5.3	4.6	5.2	3.7	3.0	-3.4	3.7	6.1	4.3	3.0	3.7
Japan	12.4	11.0	4.3	5.0	3.7	3.1	3.2	5.1	4.7	2.5	3.6
European Community[c]	4.9	4.6	2.9	3.0	0.2	0.8	1.5	2.4	2.6	2.6	2.3
France	5.9	5.4	4.0	3.6	1.2	2.5	0.7	1.4	1.7	2.1	1.6
West Germany	4.7	4.2	2.1	3.4	0.0	-1.0	1.9	3.3	2.0	2.5	1.7
Italy	4.8	6.6	2.4	3.8	1.1	0.2	0.5	3.5	2.7	2.7	2.7
United Kingdom	3.2	2.5	2.1	1.7	-1.2	1.0	3.7	2.2	3.7	2.3	3.5
Developing countries	5.3	5.8	5.7	5.0	2.2	0.9	0.5	2.8	1.7	4.0	3.3
Communist countries[d]	4.4	5.0	4.2	2.8	2.0	2.6	2.7	2.3	2.3	4.1	(e)
U.S.S.R.	4.7	5.0	3.0	2.3	1.3	2.7	3.2	1.5	0.8	3.8	1.0
Eastern Europe	3.9	3.8	4.9	1.9	-1.0	0.9	1.9	3.5	0.5	2.7	2.0
China	-0.2	8.3	5.5	6.1	4.9	8.3	9.1	12.0	12.0	7.5	9.5

[a]preliminary estimates.
[b]OECD (Organization for Economic Cooperation and Development) includes Australia, Austria, Belgium, Denmark, Finland, France, Germany, Greece, Iceland, Ireland, Italy, Luxembourg, Netherlands, New Zealand, Norway, Portugal, Spain, Sweden, Switzerland, Turkey, and United Kingdom, not shown separately.
[c]Includes Belgium, Denmark, Greece, Ireland, Luxembourg, Netherlands, Portugal, and Spain, not shown separately.
[d]Includes North Korea and Yugoslavia, not shown separately.
[e]not available.
Source: Economic Report of President 1988, p. 374.

extent. In other words, for such nations a successful productivity-enhancing measure has the nature of a public good.[9]

This sharing of the benefits from the "common pot" of technological possibilities comes about because of the interdependence of the marketplace. If, for example, the United States benefits from an innovation, industries in other nations which produce similar and competing products will be under intense pressure to imitate or obtain access to the new innovation. This is well illustrated currently by the intense competition in the automobile and pharmaceutical industries. As was stressed in Chapter 4, the penalty for failure to match innovations taking place in other countries has grown rapidly with the great increase in exports, along with the pressure of multinational firms. Timing is of the essence, since new innovations and scientific breakthroughs are broadcast throughout most of the world almost immediately.

The learning process benefits those nations that start late on the growth path. Because the lagging nation has more to learn from the leading nation than vice versa, convergence of per capita GNP takes place, since the lagging nation has more technological opportunities and can catch up with the "crowd." It should be noted that there is a serious question whether convergence will take place among the nonindustrialized poorer nations, because there is often no overlapping product mix between the poorer nation and the industrialized nations. A nation that produces no drugs cannot benefit from the latest developments in biotechnology.

But there are poorer countries where there is an overlap of product lines, as in the newly industrialized Asiatic nations: South Korea, Taiwan, Singapore, and Hong Kong. As late starters, these countries have experienced high growth rates—a pattern that is expected to continue into the future because of their links to the industrialized world. And as other nations such as Chile, Brazil, the Philippines, and Malaysia get on the industrialized bandwagon, they can take advantage of their "relative backwardness." The conditions are ripe in these nations for increasing GNP per capita at growth rates in excess of 2.5 percent.

As we discussed in Chapter 4, we can expect the industrialized nations to experience above-average per capita growth rates because of the existence of great technological opportunities on the horizon. These technological opportunities will be exploited because of intense international competition in the global marketplace. The industrialized nations will tend to experience similar growth rates because of overlapping markets. Herein lie great opportunities for poorer, nonindustrialized nations to which we turn.

GETTING ON THE GROWTH BANDWAGON: THE THIRD WORLD

If we are to forecast the future state of the international economy with reasonable accuracy, we must examine the past. To ignore the past is perilous. The past century has witnessed the economic miracle of many nations moving from a growth rate of per capita income equal to zero to a sustained positive per capita income growth rate. Max Singer[10] suggests that we can get perspective on international growth if we define "wealthy" as possessing enough resources to provide a decent living standard and a high school education to most of its citizens. In 1900 no nation could meet this requirement. Currently, roughly one-quarter of the people of the world live in nations that have met this requirement. Furthermore, when China, with one-fifth of the world's population, multiplies its per capita income of about $400 by about five times to a level of per capita income equal to about $2,000—roughly the level of Mexico, 60 percent of the world will be "wealthy." If China can achieve an annual growth rate of per capita income of 5 percent, then in 32 years—by the end of the fifth Kondratieff's period of "rise"—China will join the "wealthy" club. Given China's low level of GNP per capita, a sustained 5 percent annual growth rate of per capita income is not unreasonable, assuming the absence of political and social turbulence. For the decade 1976—1986, China's annual per capita income growth rate exceeded 5 percent.

It is lamentable that, by concentrating on the late start of India and China and on the failure of African development, we tend to get a negative view of growth in the Third World during the past century. India and China are now growing at healthy rates. Furthermore, Africa has only 11 percent of the world's population. And some African countries like Kenya and the Ivory Coast are succeeding in developing their economies.

Let us examine growth in the Third World between 1850 and 1980.[11] Crucial in understanding growth is the concept of a turning point. A turning point is the date when a nation switches from

Table 6.5
A Turning-Point Chronology

Date	Country	Date	Country	Date	Country
1840	Chile	1900	Uganda	--	Afghanistan
1850	Brazil	1900	Zimbabwe	--	Bangladesh
1850	Malaysia	1900	Tanzania	--	Ethiopia
1850	Thailand	1900	Philippines	--	Mozambique
1860	Argentina	1900	Cuba	--	Nepal
1870	Burma	1910	Korea	--	Sudan
1876	Mexico	1920	Morocco	--	Zaire
1880	Algeria	1925	Venezuela		
1880	Japan	1925	Zambia		
1880	Peru	1947	India		
1880	Sri Lanka	1947	Pakistan		
1885	Colombia	1949	China		
1895	Taiwan	1950	Iran		
1895	Ghana	1950	Iraq		
1895	Ivory Coast	1950	Turkey		
1895	Nigeria	1952	Egypt		
1895	Kenya	1965	Indonesia		

Source: Lloyd G. Reynolds, "The Spread of Economic Growth to
the Third World: 1850-1980", Journal of Economic
Literature, September, 1983, p. 958.

extensive to intensive growth. Extensive growth is experienced
when population and income are growing at the same rate, so there
is a zero rate of increase in per capita income. Intensive growth is
experienced when population grows at a slower rate than income,
so that there is a positive rate of growth of per capita income.

Table 6.5 shows data on turning points for 34 countries. The
general pattern that emerges is that most of the turning points occur
during a Kondratieff period "rise." Twenty-five turning points occur during periods of Kondratieff "rise"; nine occur during periods

of Kondratieff "decline." Thus the Kondratieff wave theory provides a powerful link between the prosperity of the Third World nations and the industrialized nations.

Let us examine the historical background relating to turning points in some detail.

The World Economic Boom—1850–1914

For the countries found in Table 6.5, median growth of per capita income from 1850 to 1914 was about 2 percent annually. During this period there was rapid economic growth in the industrialized economies of Europe and North America. This led to expanded international trade. At this time, opportunities for increased trade occurred because of higher and rising incomes in the industrialized countries. In addition, great changes in transport technology occurred to significantly lower transport costs. Among these changes were the replacement of sailing ships by steamships, the great expansion of railroads, and the completion of the Suez Canal in 1869.[12] Growth during this period was export-led. Lewis[13] found that the volume of tropical exports grew at 3.6 percent annually from 1883 to 1933.

The Longest Depression, 1914–1945

The longest depression, an apt phrase coined by W. Arthur Lewis, describes this period. This is the period of the third Kondratieff "decline," when per capita income was growing at an annual rate of only 0.6 in the United States (see Table 3.1). During this period there was a dramatic decrease in the growth rate of the volume of international trade because of the slowdown in growth and the endemic increase in tariffs and other barriers to trade. Only three countries, Venezuela, Morocco, and Zambia, joined the growth "club." (See Table 6.5.)

The Greatest Boom, 1945–1973

This period coincided roughly with the fourth Kondratieff "rise." (See Table 3.1.) During this period there was significant above-average growth of per capita income in the industrialized world and barriers to trade were reduced significantly. For this period eight countries joined the growth "club."

In reviewing these turning points, a natural question comes to the fore: Why do turning points occur? In many countries a more progressive political regime comes to power, with the regime usually believing that the goal of economic growth is important. In addition, the turning point is most often associated with a significant increase in the volume of foreign trade. This allows the nation to exploit its comparative advantage and to secure the dynamic benefits of trade which lead to increases in productivity because of international contacts. The message to the Third World country is clear: *Find political support for growth and expand trade with the rest of the world.* As Lewis put it succinctly:

For the past hundred years the rate of growth of output in the developing world has depended on the rate of growth of output in the developed world. When the developed grow fast, the developing grow fast, and when the developed slow down, the developing slow down.[14]

The record of colonialism is mixed. Some colonial powers like Japan helped initiate intensive growth in Taiwan and Korea. The United States did better than the Spanish in the Philippines. The British were also growth-minded, with the major exception of India. The results of Belgian and Portuguese rule were negative. And in some nations not under colonial rule (Ethiopia, Afghanistan, and pre–1949 China) the growth record is poor. Independence is not a magic formula for growth.

Colonial rule often established law and order and made for definite political boundaries. New export crops were introduced and an infrastructure often developed. But there were negative factors too. Often colonial governments preferred consumer goods from the home country to the detriment of local industry. And in general education was poor, with little human capital being produced.

Seventeen of the countries in Table 6.5 reached the turning point during the colonial period, while eight countries (India, Pakistan, Bangladesh, Indonesia, Egypt, Sudan, Mozambique, and Zaire) did not. Growth was not necessarily greater during the post-colonial period than during the colonial period. While 11 countries experienced more rapid growth during the post-colonial period, 3 countries had growth rates which did not differ significantly, and 6 countries experienced lower growth rates. These six countries (Burma, Cuba, Ghana, Tanzania, Uganda, and Zambia) had lower growth rates generally because of political turbulence.

THE GREAT TRANSFORMATION IN CHINA

China, with one-fifth of the world's population, is undergoing an astounding transformation. China is a poor country with a GNP per capita of about $400 in 1988. (Per capita GNP was about $16,000 in the United States in 1988.) Economic reforms instituted in 1979 have transformed China into the country with the fastest growing GNP per capita on earth between 1980 and 1985. By 1989, growth had to be reduced to contain inflation. The essence of the reforms are an expanded reliance on market forces. This signifies a transfer of power to the market and a reduction in the power of government officials. A new openness prevails, with Iaccoca's autobiography selling well, whereas Mao's book is not.

The reforms place the responsibility for managing China's collectively owned agricultural land on individual households. Under this system the government set production quotas for local communes. The individual farmers, who are members of the commune, contract to produce a share of the commune's quota. The state then sells the output at even lower prices in the urban area. The farmer is free to sell output in excess of the quota on the open market where prices are determined by supply and demand. Essentially, this is a share-cropping arrangement, with the government acting as landlord. In the short run the farmer's contract with the local commune to meet the state's quota is a fixed cost, so that output is not affected. However, in the long run it will have an adverse effect on investment decisions, with farmers reducing output because the return on capital falls. Recognizing this long-run problem, the Chinese government, in an experiment started in 1988 in two provinces, will permit state prices to rise to the level of the open market prices. There will be subsidies given to urban buyers to reduce the strain of higher prices. The growth of agricultural output in China between 1980 and 1985 expanded at a rate of 9.8 percent annually—triple the rate of increase prior to the reforms.

In industry there has been a parallel set of reforms. Under the old system, socialized firms—either state-owned or collective firms—were given quotas based upon the central plan. The state then distributed these goods at subsidized prices. Under the reforms put in place in 1978, industrial firms now operate in a system similar to the one found in agriculture. Each firm must meet the quota of output according to the government's plan, with prices set below market prices. Once the quota has been met, the firm is free to sell its remaining output in the market, with price being regulated by supply and demand.

The reforms in industry came about because of the breakdown of the central planning mechanism. For example, the central plan produced too few trucks. This resulted in a black market for trucks, with market prices for a truck in the black market being about two to three times the official price.

Firms make every effort to lower the quota of output required by the state, since market prices far exceed official prices. Firms often hide their true production capacity in order to lower the quota. Many firms simply fail to meet the state quota. Small firms find it easier to dodge the state quota, while large firms, which are easier to monitor, do not. Unfortunately, the larger firms are more efficient since their costs are lower. Thus the system perversely penalizes the efficient large firm that can take advantage of economies of scale.

Labor market controls probably hamper productivity also. Many firms—particularly foreign firms—find it difficult to find skilled workers. Workers can't change jobs unless their current employers give them permission. Many firms are unwilling to part with skilled workers, since they have borne the costs of training them.

The reforms have shifted political power from the central government to local governments. This is an ancient Chinese tradition of stressing local control because transportation and communication are difficult, particularly in the mountains of western China. Local governments have a significant impact on the allocation of resources by controlling prices and investments and by establishing barriers to trade between provinces. An example of these controls is illustrated by the problem Beijing faced when they imposed a ceiling on the price of toilet paper. As a result of the ceiling price there was a shortage of toilet paper, that is, demand exceeded supply. One solution was to raise the price, but this was rejected because it would be very unpopular with the consumer. Beijing officials instead decided to subsidize local toilet paper manufacturing. This was brilliant short-run policy, but poor long-run policy, since it would in the long run tend to produce overinvestment and overproduction of toilet paper.

If the reforms are to be effective, political power must be consistent and limited. To escape from local authority, the corporate form of business was introduced. Chinese firms, by selling stock, can dodge local controls. In 1986 a stock exchange was opened in Shanghai. There is also an infant market in government bonds. If this trend continues, China's economy will become more and more market-oriented. Whether we call this socialism or capitalism is unimportant. As China 83-year-old leader Deng Xiaoping said: "It doesn't matter if a cat is black or white, as long as it catches mice." The free market is catching mice.

China has one of the most equal distributions of income in the world. For example, doctors make little more than factory workers. With the reforms one can expect that there will be a less equal distribution of income—but with more to distribute. Like many countries, China is faced with an "equity-efficiency trade-off." The excessive pursuit of equality in the past in China inhibited growth and development. For example, since 1979 land had been divided into small plots, with each household receiving an average of 1.2 acres. This precluded the use of farm machinery. In fact, many households found farming so inefficient that they did not work the land, but worked in local industry. Now land rights may be sold to neighbors, so that the average farm is growing larger and more efficient. The result of all of this probably will be a more efficient economy, coupled with a diminished degree of equality. Efficiency and equity are substitutes.

For other countries where the income distribution is very unequal there is usually a complementarity between equity and efficiency, for example, land reform will improve efficiency and increase growth, but make incomes less unequal. It is probably reasonable to argue that a more equal distribution of income will stimulate growth in most Latin American countries.

Growth in China will be infectious. With the rising tide of Chinese growth, one would expect that it will increase growth elsewhere—at first in Asia, and later throughout the world. With a healthy rate of growth in China one can expect the more than one billion Chinese to be eager consumers for products from the rest of the world. And one can expect the Chinese genius to expand exports by exploiting market opportunities in the rest of the world. The next couple of decades hold great promise for the Chinese and her trading partners.

TWO LATE STARTERS: THE CHALLENGE MET

South Korea

South Korea is a dramatic illustration of a late starter pulling itself up from the depths. In the 1950s, South Korea was plagued by destruction wrought by the Korean War. It had a population density greater than the Netherlands, with a per capita income of only $80 in 1961.

Infrastructure was developed quickly and efficiently with American aid. Great emphasis was placed on increasing human capital through education. In addition, because of the redistribution of land, income distribution was relatively equal. Central to South Korea's development was the fact that its growth was export-led, with exports being about one-third of GNP. Real per capita GNP grew at a rate of 6.6 percent annually from 1965 to 1984. In 1986 South Korea's GNP per capita was $2,110.

Taiwan

Taiwan's growth has been spectacular. Like South Korea, its growth was export-led—having an export to GNP ration of over 50 percent, the highest in the world. Also like South Korea, it has one of the most equal distributions of income in the world. Exports raised GNP, and with the higher GNP higher tax revenues were generated. These higher tax revenues were plowed back into development spending, such as roads, and education. By 1984 it had a GNP per capita of $3,000.

Both South Korea and Taiwan have made extensive use of protection for the development of exports, citing the "infant industry" argument. However, tariffs and other barriers are being removed. For example, in 1986 the Taiwan government instituted a policy designed to reduce automobile tariffs from 65 to 35 percent over a period of five years. In 1988 automobile tariffs were reduced to 42 percent. The result has been a surge in American and European cars being sold in Taiwan.

The achievements of South Korea and Taiwan are all the more

Table 6.6
Gross National Product Per Capita of Three Divided Countries, 1985

	Market Economy	Planned Economy	Ratio of Planned to Market Economy
East Germany		$5,600	
West Germany	$10,950		0.51
North Korea		760	
South Korea	2,150		0.35
Mainland China		310	
Taiwan	3,160		0.10

Source: <u>1988 Britannica Book of the Year</u>, Encyclopedia Britannica, 1988, pp. 770-772.

impressive when they are compared with their nearby centrally planned counterparts, North Korea and Mainland China. Table 6.6 shows three pairs of nations which have shared the same culture, but which were divided politically after World War II. The centrally planned economies have a per capita GNP between 10 and 51 percent of the market-oriented economies. One cannot attribute all the difference to whether or not the economy is market-oriented or centrally planned. After World War II, Taiwan's per capita GNP was higher than Mainland China's. But North Korea's per capita GNP was higher than South Korea's after World War II. And West Germany received much more foreign aid after World War II than East Germany. Yet when all is said and done, the market economy's performance in terms of producing GNP per capita is superior to those of the centrally planned economies. Market economies have the advantage of having greater propensities to innovate and a will to enter the competitive stream of international trade. We can see this difference in terms of growth rates also, with the market-oriented growth rates being higher than the centrally planned ones. Mainland China appears to be an exception. However, it is difficult to classify Mainland China, since the reforms begun in the early 1980s have made wide use of the market.

In a comparison of Western Europe with Eastern Europe, we find that Western Europe (i.e., the European Community) had a growth rate of GNP of 1.77 percent, while the Eastern European countries had a growth rate of 1.50 percent between 1981 and 1987. (See Table 6.4.)

LATIN AMERICA: AN UNMET CHALLENGE

While recognizing the great heterogeneity of conditions, there are common problems and challenges that face most Latin American nations. The problem of faltering growth rates in Latin America is to be found within their own societies. In many Latin American countries there are arcane regulations which are designed to stifle initiative and innovation. In these countries there is an excess supply of corruption, privilege, and inefficiency. Inequalities in the distribution of income are great. These conditions are ancient, dating back to colonial times.

There is some hope for development in the large underground economy that exists. It has been estimated that half of Peru's output comes from the underground economy. In Argentina and Mexico, the underground economy may provide one-third of the national output. If these entrepreneurial energies were permitted to operate freely, legally, and in the open, there would be a significant growth in the economies of Latin America. The inescapable conclusion is that a strong dose of the free market and democracy would work wonders in Latin America.

The history of Argentina is not atypical of the Latin American malaise. Peronism emerged in the 1940s as a dominant force in Argentine politics. It centered on the charismatic figure of Juan Peron, who produced a vague blend of populism and anti-Americanism. Argentine labor unions were the main supporters of Peron, although industrialists were also favorably disposed toward him because of the prospect of protectionism. Peron proclaimed that Argentina required "economic independence," so that import substitution was the clarion call. Many industries were nationalized, and a huge public works program was undertaken, resulting in large deficits in the government's budget. In addition, foreign investment was severely restricted.

Argentina's economy, particularly the agricultural sector, has not recovered from the legacy of Peron. Argentina, with an excellent natural resource base and an educated population, has the potential to experience growth rates at the level of the industrialized countries. Yet in 1986 its GNP per capita was only $2,230, about 14 percent of the GNP per capita level in the United States. However, the election of Raul Alfonsin and the return of democracy is a hopeful sign for Argentina's future.

THE HOMOGENEITY OF TASTES AND ECONOMIES OF SCALE

Many people in low-income, developing countries decry the impact of "Westernization" of cultural values and tastes over the past century or so. The introduction of American "Italian pizza" and jeans, French wine, and Japanese electronic products disturbs their sense of propriety. This process of cultural homogenization is nothing new. The Greeks and Romans went to great lengths to impose their cultural norms wherever they had a military garrison. The Babylonian captivity of Judea had the consequence of eradicating the cultural identity of the Jews.

In the past, the imposition of culture on a conquered or subject people was accomplished mainly by force of arms. In the modern world "Westernization" has mainly taken place because of the expansion of international trade and widespread travel. In fact, if a nation wishes to maintain its cultural identity, it should prohibit trade and contact with the rest of the world. For most countries, this is too high a price to pay.

When trade takes place, one price will tend to be established for each commodity. Thus consumers throughout the international trade network face a common price structure. Furthermore, this price structure will more closely resemble that of the developed or industrialized high-income nations than that of the developing low-income nations. And, as we discussed above, per capita incomes as well as growth rates will tend to converge. Nations in the international trade network are moving in the direction of a common price structure and a common per capita income level. Given the same level of prices and incomes, we can expect the same patterns of consumption to occur.

It should be noted that we have not referred to tastes or "cultural patterns" as determinants of consumption patterns. We follow Stigler and Becker, who have argued that there is no need to resort to an exogenous factor called "tastes." For example, it is conventional among economists to argue that advertising changes tastes; Stigler and Becker argue that advertising changes prices and income:

... *all* changes in behavior are explained by changes in prices and incomes, precisely the variables that organize and give power to economic analysis. Addiction, advertising, etc. affect not tastes with the endless degrees of freedom they provide, but prices and incomes ... [15]

As international consumption patterns converge there will be unusual opportunities for firms to exploit economies of scale. For any given commodity, the size for the market will expand. For example, as the demand for canned soup expands, the firm can take advantage of economies of scale by enlarging its plant size. This will lower per unit cost of canned soup and (if there is competition) will also lower its price. Of course, if transport costs are significant, it might be constrained to locate a new plant near the market.

SUMMARY COMMENTS

In assessing the international dimension, we have found a surprising degree of economic progress in the past. At an increasing rate, more and more nations are getting on the growth bandwagon and becoming an integral part of the international trade network. Growth rates are expected to accelerate for the next two or three decades because of the international links. The expected higher growth of the industrialized developed world will be indispensable to growth rates of newly industrialized countries. Reinforcing this expectation of higher growth rates is the trend toward free trade.

At the center of the great transformation of the international economy will be the global corporation, producing and selling its wares in many different countries. The prime goal of these international corporations is to maximize profits—a goal that is not inconsistent with maximizing welfare as long as competitive conditions exist. These international corporations view the economy beyond the home country as a single market, just as an American firm in Michigan viewed the U.S. market prior to World War II. These international corporations are instrumental in making a more efficient world economy.

There may be problems for the developing countries in dealing with the global corporation. If the corporations of one industrialized nation dominate the economy of a host nation, it may be in for political trouble. To avoid this, nations which serve as host to international corporations should do so for international corporations from many different nations, so that no single industrialized nation can dominate the local economy. These international corporations should not be permitted to have the "quiet life" associated with excess market power.

NOTES

1. Adam Smith, *The Wealth of Nations* (Modern Library, New York, 1937); p. 424; originally published in 1776.

2. Angus Maddison, *Economic Growth in the West* (W. W. Norton, New York, 1964), p. 158.

3. Mercantilists were concerned with unemployment. It was believed that a favorable balance of trade would result in an increase in the money supply (i.e., an inflow of gold), thereby lowering interest rates and reducing unemployment. The policy was decidedly nationalistic, since it is impossible for all nations to have a favorable balance of trade. For a sympathetic view of the mercantilists see J. M. Keynes, *The General Theory of Employment, Interest and Money* (Harcourt, Brace, Jovanovich, New York, 1936), Chapter 23.

4. This assumes, in the main, that population and productivity growth rates are the same in all countries. In addition it assumes that the same production function is employed by all countries.

5. See Gordon W. Bertram, "Economic Growth in Canadian Industry, 1870–1915: The Staple Model and the Take-off Hypothesis," *Canadian Journal of Economics and Social Studies*, May 1963.

6. "Economic Development with Unlimited Supplies of Labor," *Manchester School of Economics and Social Studies*, May 1954.

7. *Economic Report of the President for 1988*, p. 131. Nations which have a high degree of free trade also tend to have high growth rates in per capita income. See World Bank, *World Economic Development* (Oxford University Press, Oxford, 1987).

8. All the data in the above paragraph are found in the *Economic Report of the President for 1988*. In the early 1980s farm export prices were *too high* because of the strong dollar.

9. William J. Baumol, "Productivity Growth, Convergence and Welfare: What the Long-Run Data Show," *American Economic Review*, December 1986, p. 1077.

10. "Don't Be Misled by Africa," *Wall Street Journal*, January 28, 1988, p. 17.

11. This follows Lloyd G. Reynolds, "The Spread of Economic Growth in the Third World: 1850–1980," *Journal of Economic Literature*, September 1983.

12. There is no doubt that much of the expansion of international trade in the last decade or so has been caused by the reduction in transport costs associated with the development of air freight.

13. W. Arthur Lewis, *Tropical Development, 1880–1913: Studies in Economic Progress* (Allen and Unwin, Winchester, MA., 1978).

14. W. Arthur Lewis, "The Slowing Down of the Engine of Growth," *American Economic Review* (1980), p. 555.

15. G. J. Stigler and G. S. Becker, "De Gustibuus Non Est Disputandum," *American Economic Review* (March 1977), p. 89. Emphasis in the original.

7

The End of the Malthusian Specter

I believe ... that the possibilities in the world are sufficiently great so that with the present state of knowledge, and with the additional knowledge that the human imagination and human enterprise will develop in the future, we and our descendants can manipulate the elements in such fashion that we can have all the mineral raw materials we need and desire at prices ever smaller relative to other prices and to our total incomes. ... So has it been in the past, and therefore so it is likely to be in the future.[1]

In previous chapters we have examined various causes for the expected acceleration in the growth rate of per capita GNP. Among these factors are the acceleration of technological advance (Chapter 4), favorable structural changes in the U.S. economy (Chapter 5), and the integration of the world economy (Chapter 6). Here we focus on population growth, putting the quietus on demographic pessimism. Malthus's contention that an unconstrained stork will drive nations into misery and poverty is far off the mark. Population growth will not sabotage the process by which GNP per capita grows in the United States and the world. In fact, population trends complement the trend toward higher per capita growth rates throughout the world. There is no "population bomb."

EMPIRICAL SURVEY OF POPULATION TRENDS

An examination of Table 7.1, which shows population trends since 1960, indicates the following:

Table 7.1

World Population Annual Growth by Continent and Region 1960 to 1986 (percent)

Continent and Region	1960–1965	1965–1970	1970–1975	1975–1980	1980–1986
World	1.9	2.1	2.0	1.7	1.7
More developed regions	1.2	0.9	0.9	0.7	0.6
Less developed regions	2.3	2.5	2.4	2.1	2.0
Africa	2.4	2.5	2.6	2.8	2.8
Asia	2.1	2.4	2.3	1.8	1.7
Latin America	2.8	2.7	2.5	2.3	2.3
North America	1.5	1.1	1.1	1.1	0.9
Europe	0.9	0.7	0.6	0.4	0.3
Soviet Union	1.5	1.0	0.9	0.9	0.9
Australia and New Zealand	2.0	1.9	1.7	1.0	1.2

Source: <u>Statistical Abstract</u>, 1987, p. 814. From U.S. Bureau of Census World Population Profile, 1985.

1. World population growth rates reached a peak about 1970, with population growing at 2 percent.

2. The more developed regions of the world generally show low and falling growth rates—in the neighborhood of 1 percent.

3. The less developed regions of the world also show declining growth rates. Growth rates of population are two to three times the growth rates of population of the more-developed regions of the world.

4. Africa is a major exception to the declining population growth rates with its rate rising from 2.4 percent in 1960 to 1965 to 2.8 percent in 1980 to 1986.

FACTORS LIMITING POPULATION AND THEIR IMPLICATION FOR ECONOMIC GROWTH

Family size is related to per capita income in a typical developing country. Initially, an increase in income will generate a larger family size, with a typical family having more income to support a larger family. Other factors that increase family size—factors which are related to higher incomes—are improved nutrition and health conditions, as well as significant reductions in infant mortality.

But as family income increases further, the desired family size falls so that there is a negative relationship between per capita GNP and population growth.[2] The benefit-cost ratio of children declines as growth takes place for a variety of reasons. (1) The family has shifted from an agrarian to an urban setting. Children as workers on the farm are more valuable than when the family is located in the city. (2) As GNP per capita grows, in many countries a formal public social security system is developed and supplants the informal social security system of the extended family where children took care of parents in their old age. Therefore, children have less value as providers of security for their parents. (3) With higher income levels, the cost of a child will increase. This is because the production and rearing of a child is labor-intensive. With wages rising with economic growth, the opportunity cost of time rises, thereby increasing the cost of children. Other factors will determine the size of the family. Among these are: the level of taxation as it relates to family size, the development of a "women's liberation" movement with women increasingly moving into the formal labor market, and the availability of contraceptive devices.

The impact of these factors can be seen in China's recent experience. China has experienced a remarkable success in controlling population, limiting families to one child. With 21 percent of the world's population, it had a population growth rate of 1 percent annually for the 1980 to 1986 period. China's birth rate declined from 39 in 1960 to 19 in 1982. By 1982, almost three-quarters of Chinese married women were practicing contraception—a rate higher than in the United States. The Chinese have successfully utilized economic measures, with nine provinces using a "baby" tax on couples producing more than two children. Typically, wages are reduced by 5 to 10 percent with the birth of a third child, with the tax rate rising with the number of children. Strong social pressures are brought to bear through neighborhood and factory groups to ensure that couples adhere to the rule of having no more than one child. Successful programs for population planning and limitation have been experienced by Singapore and Indonesia, with the former using economic incentives extensively and the latter using social pressures. Singapore reversed its policies in the 1980s and is now encouraging population growth. Programs with less success are found in Pakistan and India.

As per capita GNP increases and family size is reduced, certain structural changes in the economy occur. These changes reinforce our forecast that GNP per capital will grow at a significantly higher rate than in the past. Here we witness again a benign circle.

The Minimal Impact of Diminishing Returns

The problem associated with diminishing returns will be minimized if population growth is moderated. An increase in the labor force resulting from an increase in population with a fixed capital stock results in a reduction in GNP per capita. This occurs because there is less capital per worker, with the capital stock spread more thinly among the workers. This reduces the workers' marginal product because of the law of diminishing returns. Economists have found that, roughly speaking, a 1 percent increase in the labor force, other things being equal, will reduce GNP per capita by 0.3 percent. With a reduction in the growth rate of population and labor force expected over the next few decades, the law of diminishing returns will be unimportant in taking its toll on per capita GNP.

Some economists emphasize that population growth can produce economies of scale—where we experience greater efficiency and lower costs associated with large-scale production. These economists emphasize that economies of scale more than offset diminishing returns. For example, Simon argues:

A bigger population implies a bigger market, all else equal. A bigger market promotes bigger manufacturing plants that likely are more efficient than smaller ones, as well as longer production runs and hence lower setup costs per unit of output.... A larger market also makes possible a greater division of labor and hence an increase in the skill with which goods and services are made.... A bigger population makes profitable many major social investments that would not otherwise be profitable—for example, railroads, irrigation systems, and ports.[3]

The argument for enlarging population size to take advantage of economies of scale would make sense in a world characterized by autarky. However, with international trade flourishing and expected to be increasingly open in the future, the argument is misplaced. Taiwan does not have to increase its population to enjoy economies of scale because the world is practically the marketplace for Taiwan's output.

The Savings Rate Will Increase

As the family size decreases, the rate of savings increases. For example, it was found that the marginal propensity to save out of per capita income—the ratio of a change in saving to the change in income—was 0.35 to 0.40 for 6 richer Latin American countries (Argentina, Chile, Cuba, Panama, Uruguay, and Venezuela) but was 0.20 for 14 poorer Latin American countries.[4] If a nation saves more, interest rates will be reduced and investment in new innovations will be stimulated. In addition, with fewer children of school age, government may absorb less of the available savings, since there is less need to invest in school facilities. Alternatively, it may increase the quality of education. In other words, the "crowding out" problem—where government spending forces a reduction in private investment spending—will be less severe as the size of the family is reduced.

However, one should note the dissenting view of J. A. Schumpeter, who believes that the small family will tend to reduce the savings rate.[5] In addition, we have assumed that there will be no problem in absorbing savings since we are oriented toward the long run. There may be Keynesian episodes of significant unemployment in the short run where one would want to discourage savings and encourage consumption because of the existence of large-scale unemployment. But these episodes should be fairly rare because of the reduced amplitude of the business cycle expected.[6]

The Burden of Dependency Will Diminish

As population grows, the age composition of the population changes. If population grows slowly, no age group dominates. This means that there are more people in the working age group of 15 to 65 than there are below 15 and above 65. If population grows rapidly, there is often a dramatic increase in the number of children, particularly if there is a significant reduction in infant mortality. Typically, in low-income countries about 45 percent of the population is in the dependent age brackets of less than 15 years old or over 65 years of age. In the high-income developed countries the dependency bracket is about 30 to 35 percent of population. Thus, with a lower growth rate of population throughout most of the world, we can expect the percentage of dependent population to decrease. Put differently, a larger labor force with a given population will enhance the growth rate of GNP per capita.

A lower rate of population growth will probably increase the population over 65 and may increase the dependency ratio some. In 1981, only 18 percent of males 65 years of age and older were in the labor force. Incentives to retire early are built into the Social Security system, with the penalty for early retirement being small.

However, this incentive to retire early will be weakened in the United States by the provision to increase benefits from 3 to 8 percent over a 20-year period for each year of delay in retirement, beginning in 1990. In addition, the age of full social security eligibility will be increased from age 65 to 67 by the year 2027. And it should be noted that many older people who retire find other work (often in the underground economy), so that the retirement data exaggerate the extent of early exit from the labor force. Retirement incentives will be reduced further when the penalty for social security recipients working will probably be eliminated in the near future. Finally, improved health care will reduce the desire for early retirement. All in all, the growth of the older retired population appears to be greatly exaggerated for the future.

The Quality of the Labor Force Will Increase

There is a very important qualitative dimension to family size. The cost of a child rises as economic growth takes place because of the increase in wages which increases the cost of time—in effect, increasing the cost of a child. When the cost of a child increases there is a reduction in the quantity but an increase in the quality of children demanded, as measured by the income-earning potential when the child reaches adulthood. This rise in the quality of children occurs because there are fewer children to absorb resources.[7] If the price of investing in the quality of the child rises, such as an increase in the price of food, health care, or education, the family will probably decrease the demand for quality. It follows that a smaller population growth rate and smaller family size mean a more productive labor force so that the effective labor force grows faster than the population growth rate. This in turn will contribute to increasing the growth rate of GNP per capita.

To this point we have focused on the problem of excess population. Some analysts and politicians are concerned with the problems associated with a declining population. In the province of Quebec the fertility rate is 1.4, compared with 1.7 for Canada and 1.8 for the United States. This extremely low fertility rate has led to fears that the political power of the French-speaking province will be diluted. As a result, the Quebec government passed a series of measures aimed at boosting the birthrate. These measures will provide 3,000 Canadian dollars for every additional child, beginning with the third child. These allowances will continue until the child reaches two years of age. In addition, there will be income tax cuts for families bearing three or more children. Other countries such as West Germany, France, Sweden, and Singapore have also developed policies to increase the fertility rate. Singapore in the 1970s had a policy of discouraging fertility.

SUMMARY

Empirical evidence is clear that economic growth is a powerful force in limiting population growth, once a threshold family income level is reached. Demographic patterns as well as demographic evolution in most parts of the world in the next few decades appear to be complementary to the goal of increased rate of growth of GNP per capita. The slowing of the rate of population growth will tend to increase the savings rate, reduce the dependency ratio, and improve the quality of the labor force—with the net result being additional growth in GNP per capita. All of this is summarized in Figure 7.1.

Figure 7.1
The Benign Circle of Income and Population Growth

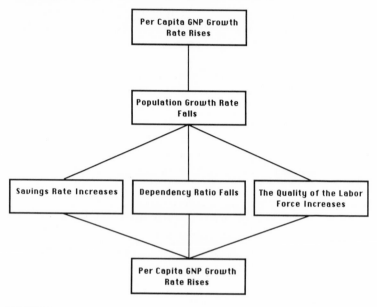

NOTES

1. Julian Simon, *The Ultimate Resource* (Princeton University Press, 1981), p. 41.

2. There is fairly strong empirical evidence that the relationship between family income and family size is negative after a threshold income level is reached. See: R. A. Easterlin, "The Economics and Sociology of Fertility: A Synthesis," Paper prepared for *Seminar in Early Industrialization*, Princeton, 1972. Adelman statistically estimated the relation between birth rates and per capita income for 37 countries in the 1947–1957 period (Irma Adelman, "An Econometric Analysis of Population Growth," *American Economic Review* (June 1963), p. 321). She found that, if the age of the mother was between 20 and 24, a 10 percent increase in per capita income would increase the birth rate by 2 percent. These results reflect in part the positive relationship between family income and family size when income levels are low. In addition, it is difficult to disentangle per capita income from other variable influencing family size, since other variables are closely correlated with income levels. She found that the birth rate falls with the percentage employed outside agriculture, the higher the educational levels, and with population density.

3. Simon, *Ultimate Resource*, pp. 203–25.

4. Raymond F. Mikesell and James E. Zinser, "The Nature of the Savings Function in Developing Countries: A Survey of the Theoretical and Empirical Literature," *The Journal of Economic Literature* (March 1973), p. 6.

5. J. A. Schumpeter, *Capitalism, Socialism and Democracy* (Harper & Row, New York, 1947), p. 161.

6. See pp. 136–41.

7. There is some evidence that when an additional child arrives the mother will eventually enter the labor force to increase family income, giving up household work or leisure. Thus family income is not necessarily fixed.

8

Government Policy

*...we should not expect the appropriate or optimum rate of indus-
trial output to be constant, but to be subject to a succession of what
may be called "justifiable" increases and decreases ... some of which
are of a fairly rhythmical nature.*[1]

Government policy may be a powerful force in improving the performance of the economy. However, in approaching the topic of
government policy, we are immediately faced with the fact that
economists do not speak with one voice. Rather, opinions and
conclusions among economists are frequently at odds with one
another. Perhaps this is exaggerated by the fact that controversies
among economists are given much more attention by the media
than agreements. Still there are a great many differences among
economists. There are three main causes for these differences.

First, economists may differ with regard to *value judgments*. Differences in value judgments often come to light when there is a
trade-off or conflict between different goals. For example, it is commonly concluded by economists that there is a short-run trade-off
between the rate of inflation and the rate of unemployment, known
as the Phillips curve. The Phillips curve indicates that, if the rate
of unemployment is to be reduced, this will frequently require an
increase in the rate of inflation. Economist A may believe a 6 percent
rate of unemployment and a 2 percent rate of inflation is optimal.

Economist B, on the other hand, may hold that a 5 percent rate of unemployment and a 4 percent rate of inflation is optimal. Here the difference between the two economists is found in their different value judgments: Economist A believes avoiding inflation is more important than avoiding unemployment, while economist B believes the opposite. These value judgments are personal and their validity cannot be evaluated scientifically.

These differences may evaporate in the long run, with both economists concluding that there is no long-run trade-off between inflation and unemployment. That is, a wide range of inflation rates are possible at a given rate of unemployment. It follows that if the trade-off between inflation and unemployment disappears, value judgments are *not* an important source of difference among economists. In fact, we argued above that goals which are in conflict in the short run are often complementary in the long run. For example, a policy which supports the acceleration of technological progress will work in the direction of minimizing *both* unemployment and the rate of inflation in the long run.

A second source of conflict among economists may result because of *theoretical differences*. Economist X may believe that an increase in the money supply will raise the price level in the short run, while economist Y believes an increase in the money supply will increase real GNP. Economists X and Y now differ because they use different models. Again, the difference between X and Y is more significant in the short run than in the long run because there is more theoretical agreement in the long run than in the short run.

A third source of conflict among economists may result from *empirical differences*. Even if there is no dispute over values or over theoretical models of how the economy operates, there may still be a dispute over the magnitude of the response to different policies. For example, economist D may favor an investment tax credit because he believes it will have a substantial impact on increasing investment. On the other hand, economist E may look with disfavor on an investment tax credit because she believes it will have a minor impact on increasing investment. Differences with regard to estimates of empirical values among economists appear to be less important in the long run than in the short run because full adjustment is made in the long run. In the short run, adjustment to an investment tax credit takes time and empirical work is bedeviled by the fact that the full effects of policy are not completed. Fundamental long-term ratios such as the savings-income ratio, the capital-output ratio, the money-nominal GNP ratio, the capital-labor ratio, and the labor income-GNP ratio are much more stable in the long run than the short run.[2]

In summary, the three different sources of conflict among economists—value judgments, theoretical judgments, and empirical judgments—tend to be significantly less important as we go from the short run to the long run. What follows focuses mainly on short- and long-run macroeconomic policies that a large number of economists probably hold. These policies will support private activity in generating and sustaining high economic growth rates over the next two or three decades. The discussion that follows is mainly relevant to the United States and other highly industrialized nations.

SHORT-RUN MACROECONOMIC POLICY

In a dynamic economy, real GNP is inherently subject to short-term fluctuations. These fluctuations in real GNP will be associated with variations in the price level and the rate of unemployment. Within wide limits, macroeconomic policy should be passive and leave the economy alone. In a growing economy, this would require that the money supply increase at a steady rate. If the money supply were to grow at a rate equal to the rate of increase in real GNP, the price level would not vary significantly. Furthermore, the government budget should be balanced, with tax revenues equaling government expenditures.

When there are serious deviations from full employment without inflation, an active monetary and/or fiscal policy is called for. The definition of "serious" here not only depends on economic analysis but on one's ideological predilections. To illustrate, suppose we considered a rate of inflation in excess of 6 percent and an unemployment rate of 7 percent as "serious." From 1970 to 1988, the unemployment and/or inflation rate exceeded the limits 12 out of 18 years. This means an active policy would be employed two-thirds of the time. If we set the upper limit at 7 percent for both the unemployment and inflation rates, this would require an active policy 7 out of 18 years. If, as argued above, the rate of growth accelerates and the business cycle is shallower, the unemployment and inflation problems should be less serious than in the past. Therefore we may expect much less need for active short-term policy in the future.

If there is serious unemployment without inflation, an easy money and/or an easy fiscal policy is called for. And if there is serious inflation without unemployment, a tight money and/or a tight fiscal policy is called for. But what if the nation suffers from stagflation, where there is serious inflation *and* unemployment? The precise combination of monetary and fiscal policy depends on the comparative advantage of each policy tool.

On empirical grounds it appears that variations in the money supply are relatively more successful in combating excessive inflation than in combating excessive unemployment and fiscal policy is relatively more successful in combating unemployment than in combating inflation. During the early 1980s, the United States suffered from stagflation—excessive unemployment and excessive inflation. A tight monetary policy and an easy fiscal policy were pursued.[3] From a short-run view, the policy is stable and produced the right results, with inflation and unemployment decreasing. However, from the longer-run perspective, this policy combination flirts with disaster. Higher interest rates produce a bias against investment. The reduced investment relative to GNP in turn reduces the growth rate of GNP as well as the productivity of the economy. In addition, this policy combination increased the value of the dollar and increased the deficit in the balance of trade. Fortunately, since about 1985 this policy has been reversed, with the money supply growing more rapidly and the deficit being reduced.[4]

Short-term policy, particularly fiscal policy, is bedeviled by the problems of timing. Congressional action to vary taxes and/or expenditures is a slow and cumbersome process. For example, it took over a year from the time it was proposed to *decrease* taxes in 1964 and to *increase* taxes in 1968. Furthermore, the typical member of Congress is primarily concerned with conditions in his or her own district. Complicating matters further, most members of Congress find it politically congenial to increase expenditures and lower taxes. Reducing expenditures or increasing taxes is the recipe for political suicide. The president is perhaps the one politician on the national level who can effectively take a national (and perhaps international) view of the state of the economy. This suggests that fiscal policy can be significantly improved by giving the president discretionary power to vary taxes and expenditures by, say, 5 percent of the levels authorized by Congress. This would improve the timing of fiscal policy and limit the congressional bias of producing deficits.

Short-run macroeconomic policy can probably be improved if nominal wage rates are more flexible. Currently, the three-year labor-management contract is dominant, making the nominal wage rate less flexible. Perhaps we should make it illegal to have labor-management contracts in excess of one year. Thus, if the economy slipped into a recession, modest reductions in the nominal wage rate (or reductions in the rate of increase in the nominal wage rate) would be a significant antirecession policy, complementing monetary and fiscal policy.

Martin Weitzman[5] has argued that wages could be made more flexible by more extensive use of profit-sharing plans. For example, workers would receive about 80 percent of their income in wages, with 20 percent on average taking the form of a bonus. The bonus would exceed 20 percent during a period of full employment when profits are high and would fall below 20 percent during a period of unemployment when profits are low. The bonus system seems to be working well in Japan, where it is common for 25 percent of labor compensation to take the form of a bonus.[6]

Many other policies can be proposed to improve the short-run operation of the economy. Serious consideration should be given to measures which will reduce structural unemployment. For example:

1. Improve the quality of employment information provided by U.S. Employment Service.
2. Link education (particularly at the high school level) more directly with the labor market by placing greater emphasis on on-the-job training.
3. Provide partial moving allowance for unemployed workers who move from areas of unemployment to get a job.

In addition, we should improve the built-in stabilizers, or consider reducing the impact of built-in destabilizers. For example, taxes to support the unemployment compensation system usually increase when unemployment increases. While this type of taxing may have some justification at the micro level, it unfortunately contributes to macroeconomic instability.

No single policy is capable of stabilizing the economy in the short run. But a monetary policy coordinated with fiscal policy and complemented by a flexible wage policy can make a significant contribution to the short-run health of the economy.

LONG-RUN MACROECONOMIC POLICY

Government policy should generally try to encourage savings and investment. With higher rates of savings and investment, the quantity and quality of capital per worker will increase. The consequence will be higher productivity, higher GNP levels, and higher growth rates of GNP. Two broad guidelines should be kept in mind:

1. *Keep tax rates as low as possible.* If taxes are minimized, the rate of return on savings and investment will be increased because of the higher rate of return after taxes. To minimize taxes requires that the government restrict its activities to areas where it has a comparative advantage. In general, government should undertake only those activities which have benefits greater than costs, and where the government benefit-cost ratio significantly exceeds the benefit-cost ratio of the private economy. Many activities of government today cannot pass this test and are a burden on the economy.

2. *Keep the tax system as neutral as possible.* Taxes potentially distort and misallocate resources in a competitive economy. If we tax industry A, but subsidize industry B, we will get too little output from industry A and too much from industry B. Assuming the two industries are competitive, it is probably best to tax both industries at the same rate.[7]

Let us turn to specifics regarding savings and investment.

The Rate of Savings

It is repeated ad nauseam that American must save more. However, Americans are not as profligate as pictured. The *gross private* savings rate (personal savings plus gross corporate savings) has remained at 15 to 17 percent of GNP through the 1960s and 1970s into the 1980s. There is no downward or upward trend. However, the composition of savings has changed, with retained earnings and capital consumption allowances increasing while the savings rate by households has apparently decreased. The reason for this change in the composition of savings is that the composition of *investment* has changed. Investment has shifted to shorter-lived assets, leading to an increase in depreciation allowances. This change in the composition of savings reflects changes in the tax law which changed the composition of *investment* (i.e., the introduction of the tax credit along with the widespread use of accelerated depreciation) rather than a change in the savings rate.

In fact, the *personal* savings rate of the United States is probably underestimated. In 1987 the reported data show that the Japanese had a personal savings rate almost four times that of the United States. Kenichi Ohmae[8] concludes that the reported data on personal savings in the United States and Japan cannot be compared. After adjusting for different statistical methods. such as the treatment of public pensions and consumer durables, Ohmae concludes that Americans and the Japanese have about the same rate of personal savings.

Even if savings rates by Americans are too low, we should recognize that if there is significant unemployment, investment can be sustained by using unemployed resources. With unemployed resources, an increase in investment may be largely self-financed. An increase in investment increases GNP *and* savings. Furthermore, much of the recent discussion of the adequacy of savings ignores the fact that foreign savings are potentially available for use in the United States. Equilibrium does not require that domestic savings equal domestic investment. In 1987, private savings in the United States were about $43 billion less than private investment.

Assuming full employment, an increase in savings will lower interest rates and increase the amount of investment. An increase in investment in turn will increase the rate of technological change, thereby increasing the rate of growth of GNP. It is commonly argued that cutting tax rates on savings will increase the rate of savings.

One approach is to lower the progressivity of the personal income tax. Since the upper-income households do most of the savings, this would increase the after-tax rate of return on savings. This will *probably* increase the rate of savings. Another approach would be to make use of a broadly based federal excise tax to supplant the federal income tax. This would mean that the return on savings would go untaxed. With a higher after-tax return the rate of savings will *probably* increase.

However, note that we have said that an increase in the after-tax return on savings will probably increase savings. This requires qualification. An increase in the rate of return for the saver will increase the rate of savings because of the "substitution effect," that is, savings will increase because of the higher return on savings. However, the "income effect"—higher interest rates increase the income of the saver—will increase consumption and reduce savings. If the magnitude of the "income effect" is greater than that of the "substitution effect," the rate of savings will fall. Empirical evidence on the relationship between interest rates adjusted for taxes and the rate of savings is uncertain.[9]

A reduction in government (federal, state, and local) deficits will increase national savings if it does not reduce private savings by the same amount. Some economists have concluded that an increase in taxes would be fully offset by a decrease in private savings, so that national savings would not increase.[10] This occurs because a current increase in taxes signifies that future tax liabilities will be lower. With lower future tax liabilities, there is less need to save. Empirical studies have rejected the idea of a complete offset of private savings by public savings.

The Rate of Investment

Investment is determined mainly by the real rate of interest (nominal rate of interest less the expected rate of inflation) and the level of taxation. Let us examine these two factors as they affect investment.

The degree of capital intensity depends on the interest rate relative to the wage rate. If the interest rate falls relative to the wage rate, investment will increase. One possible indirect route to increase investment would be to encourage savings. An increase in the savings rate will lower interest rates relative to wage rates and stimulate investment. Another route to directly increase investment is to increase the wage rate, holding the interest rate constant. A union which raises wage rates of its members above the competitive level is implicitly engaging in a policy to stimulate investment. For example, John L. Lewis, as head of the United Mine Workers, secured wages above the competitive level. These relatively high wage rates no doubt were a major cause for the high degree of mechanization of American coal mines.

It must be stressed that investment is determined by the real rate of interest—not the nominal rate of interest. For example, if an investor purchases a machine for $100 when the nominal rate of interest is 10 percent, but also expects the rate of inflation to be 7 percent, the real rate of interest is 3 percent. The investor expects the price of the machine to increase by 7 percent (equal to the expected rate of inflation), so that he benefits from a capital gain. The *net* cost of funds is 3 percent.

Two extreme examples, where real rates of interest differ significantly from nominal rates of interest, may reinforce this point. In 1932 nominal yields on corporate bonds were about 5 percent. But the price level was falling by about 10 percent. If we equate the rate of deflation with the expected rate of deflation, the real corporate bond rate equaled 15 percent. These high real rates of interest help to explain the very low rate of investment in 1932. Another example is the situation in 1980. Nominal mortgage rates were about 13 percent, but since the actual rate of inflation (again assumed to equal the expected rate of inflation) was also rising by 13 percent, real mortgage rates were zero! The 13 percent nominal interest rate was offset by the expected 13 percent increase in house values. And home sales were brisk in 1980 even though nominal mortgage rates were at record levels.

If nominal rates of interest are adjusted to reflect the rate of inflation, real rates of interest will tend to be constant. As a result, investment will be independent of the rate of inflation. This might lead one to conclude that the rate of inflation is of no significance for investment. However, in the short run the adjustment to the nominal interest rate to reflect the inflation rate is partial, so that real rates of interest will vary. The two illustrations in 1932 and 1980, given in the previous paragraph, illustrate the partial adjustment of real interest rates. Furthermore, there is evidence that the higher the *actual* rate of inflation the greater the uncertainty about the *expected* rate of inflation. This increased uncertainty will raise the minimum required rate of return on investment, thereby inhibiting investment. A reasonable policy would probably be to keep the rate of inflation as stable as possible, averaging zero.

In making an investment, the firm is concerned with the rate of return on an investment *after taxes*. Lower tax rates on investment income will increase the rate of investment. For example, lower corporate tax rates will stimulate investment. A policy which permits firms to accelerate depreciation or to shorten the depreciation period will increase the present value of cash flows and stimulate investment. The investment tax credit, which permitted firms to take a tax credit of 10 percent, in effect reduced the price of capital goods and stimulated investment. The Tax Reform Act of 1986 eliminated the tax credit.

The 1986 tax law will have a profound effect on investment patterns in years to come. The precise impact of the change in the tax law on the level of investment is very difficult to estimate. By lowering marginal corporate tax rates (from 0.46 to 0.34) as well as marginal personal income tax rates, investment will be stimulated. But investment will be decreased because of the elimination of the 10 percent tax credit, the elimination of the preferential rates on capital gains, and the extension of depreciation periods. By eliminating the special treatment accorded different types of investment resulting from the tax credit and the preferential rates on capital gains, the pattern of investment will be more rational.

It is unfortunate that the 1986 tax law did not put an end to the double taxation of corporate dividends. The corporation pays a tax on corporate profits, and when dividends are declared the stockholder pays a personal income tax on dividends received. This feature of the law is discriminatory against the corporate form of enterprise. Double taxation could be eliminated completely by imputing all corporate profits to the stockholder. Thus a dollar of corporate profits would be considered part of the personal income of the stockholder. This would eliminate the need for a corporate tax.

Frequent changes in tax laws add to the uncertainty experienced by the firm. In the 1960s and 1970s there were about 10 to 12 significant changes in tax laws. And in the 1980s there has been a a major tax law change every year. Uncertain tax policies make investment choices by the firm more difficult. Increased uncertainty associated with frequent changes in the tax laws leads the firm to invest in tax shelters and to spend on tax-deductible items.

LONG-RUN INDUSTRIAL POLICY: MUCH ADO ABOUT NOTHING?

The current debate on whether or not the United States should have an industrial policy is as old as the nation. Alexander Hamilton in his "Report on Manufactures" recommended that tariffs be imposed on imports in order to aid "infant"[a] industries. These arguments for protective tariffs were further refined by the German economist Frederich List as appropriate policy in Germany. The counterarguments by John Stuart Mill essentially asserted that these arguments were logical, but support for "infant" industries would be difficult to apply in practice.

Current proponents argue that industrial policies are required along with other policies (e.g., improvements in education) if the United States is to regain its competitive preeminence. Industrial policies of the nation are akin to strategic planning for the firm. They are the basic instrument for maximizing national economic growth. Industrial polices involve an exchange of views between private industry and government in setting up national goals. Perhaps the French experience in using "indicative planning" and the Japanese experience with its Ministry of Industry and Trade (MITI) serve as prototypes for industrial policies.

Generally, industrial policies involve three different but closely related policies.

1. A public body would be established to partially finance civilian medium-term industrial research on new products and processes. Projects would be selected on the basis of peer review in much the same way that the National Science Foundation operates in awarding research funds to universities.[11]

2. The government would search for ways to reduce costs for industrial firms. For example, government would permit consultation by firms in the same industry on research and development in order to avoid duplication of effort. These firms would be exempt from antitrust action.

3. The government would develop a systematic approach to the problem of "industrial triage." In the case of declining industries, the government would agree to provide protection from foreign competition on condition that the industry be restructured to make it more lean and efficient to meet foreign competition. In making loans to industries or firms in difficulty, the government would become a part owner or creditor of the firm.

Clearly the United States has had, and continues to have, an informal industrial policy. Government policy aims to guide private industry with the goal of stimulating growth. A partial list of governmental policies that are elements of an industrial policy are:

1. Financial support by New York for the building of the Erie Canal.
2. Establishment of the Rural Electrification Administration to provide low-cost electricity.

3. Establishment of the Export-Import Bank to offer subsidized loans to stimulate exports.

4. Establishment of the Federal National Mortgage Association to provide a secondary market for mortgages.

5. Establishment of the Commodity Credit Corporation to give loans to farmers.

6. Development of a network of agricultural research through the Department of Agriculture and the state universities.

7. Establishment of the Small Business Administration.

The argument between those supporting and those opposed to an industrial policy is one of degree. One can argue that some past efforts have been failures, such as the policies of the Small Business Administration. On the other hand, even if one is ideologically bound to laissez-faire, some of these policies can be justified because of market failure. Thus the provision of financial support for research in the areas of agriculture, space, and defense can be justified on economic grounds since the researcher cannot appropriate the benefits of his or her research findings. Without government support, the research would not be done even though the benefits exceed costs.

Some economists object to these programs because they feel the market, with all of its imperfections, is a more effective instrument for providing direction for the economy than a policy of the "seen hand" of government. In spite of good intentions, many government programs too often get mired in parochial and partisan politics and do not serve the national interest.

In fact, the Reagan administration, often pictured as an opponent of industrial policy, has had an industrial policy. Some examples from 1987 alone:

1. The White House called for a broad program to develop superconducting material. In addition, constraints on antitrust laws will be relaxed to permit firms to collaborate on research.

2. The Reagan administration approved a $4.4 billion plan to build a supercollider.

3. The Reagan administration proposed funding a high-performance computer strategy.

4. Contracts were awarded for building the first permanent space station.

This, of course, is only a sample from one year. Robert B. Reich, often called the guru of industrial policy as well as a critic of the Reagan administration, concluded:

One of the Reagan Administration's enduring legacies will be the foundation of a national industrial policy.... Rarely has an Administration sought more actively to encourage specific industries and technologies. Never has an Administration so often justified its interventions by appeals to American competiveness. And to think that just a few years ago the idea of a national industrial policy was controversial![12]

The debate on industrial policy has come full circle and is closed.

A CATEGORICAL IMPERATIVE: DO NOT HARM

There are many other policies besides macroeconomic policy through which government can make a significant contribution toward economic progress if it concentrates on areas where it has a significant comparative advantage. Government can also make a significant contribution to economic progress by *not* concentrating on areas where it does *not* have a comparative advantage. Clearly, government has a function in providing for the national defense as well as law and order. In addition, the provision of much infrastructure such as education, environmental controls, and roads will normally be provided by government. Laws should not be changed too frequently. Frequent changes in the law produce a residue of uncertainty which inhibits economic activity. Let us contrast a beneficial and a harmful law.

A beneficial legal provision is illustrated by the Patent Restoration Act of 1984. This was the first change in the patent law since 1861. Under this law, pharmaceutical patents will be increased up to five years, depending on the clinical and testing time required. The need for extending the legal life of a patent was recognized because the clinical testing time and the review time by the Food and Drug Administration (FDA) were often prolonged. In fact, the effective or economic life of a drug patent was about one-half of the 17-year legal life. In addition, a generic company producing the same drug has only to demonstrate to the FDA that the drug is equivalent to the pioneering firm's product. Previously the generic firm had to replicate the expensive and time-consuming clinical tests performed by the pioneer firm. If the effective patent life can be extended beyond 3 years to a total of 20 years of patent production, it will probably stimulate research and development in the pharmaceutical industry. At the same time it will encourage a much quicker diffusion of new innovations in the industry.[13]

In contrast to the 1984 drug act, the government can diminish the growth potential of the economy. Under Congressional mandate, Alaskan crude oil cannot be exported. So the crude oil is forced to take the very long journey from Alaska to the Gulf of Mexico. Under the Jones Act of 1920, only high-cost U.S. tankers can carry Alaskan crude oil. Once it gets to the western side of Panama, the crude is unloaded and sent through an 80-mile pipeline to the eastern side of Panama. It is then reloaded onto another U.S. tanker for shipment to U.S. Gulf Coast refineries.

It is estimated that shipping Alaskan crude oil to Japan would cost about 50 cents a barrel compared to $3.50 for shipping Alaskan crude oil to the Gulf Coast. If there were no restrictions on exporting Alaskan crude oil, it would be exported to Japan (replacing the more expensive imports from the Middle East) and the United States would import oil from Mexico (replacing the more expensive oil from Alaska). Further benefits would be had if the Jones Act was eliminated.

Many other examples of harmful governmental policies can be given, from wasteful pork barrel projects to farm subsidies and to quotas imposed on imports. Government policy should not respond to every problem that appears on the landscape.

NOTES

1. D. H. Robertson, *Banking Policy and the Price Level* (Augustus M. Kelley, New York, 1949), p. 18.

2. Lawrence Klein, *An Introduction to Econometrics* (Prentice-Hall, Englewood Cliffs, NJ, 1962), p. 183.

3. The deficit was the result of miscalculations by both President Reagan and the Congress. By cutting taxes, President Reagan felt that Congress would be forced to cut expenditures. But Congress balked at reducing

expenditures. However, many members of Congress believed that a vote for cutting tax rates would not increase the deficit because lower tax *rates* would not decrease tax *revenues*. A cut in tax rates will increase the return to the factors of production, thereby enlarging the tax base. Tax revenues—tax rates times the tax base—would not decrease because the tax base would increase by a percentage at least equal to the percentage cut in tax rates. While this proposition has some academic respectability, it is, as events have shown, empirically flawed when applied at the macro level.

4. We should be aware of many qualifications and disagreements with this brief account of macroeconomic policy. In a world of uncertainty, there have been doubts raised about aiming to have the money supply grow at a constant rate. If there is great uncertainty about the supply and demand for money. it may be more appropriate to aim to achieve a constant real rate of interest. With regard to fiscal policy, some economists argue that at full employment there should be a surplus in the government's budget, while others argue that there should be a deficit. For details see Robert J. Gordon, *Macroeconomics*, 3rd ed., (Little, Brown, Boston, 1984), pp. 460–64. There are also economists who believe the budget should be balanced year in and year out.

5. Martin Weitzman, *The Share Economy* (Harvard University Press, Cambridge, Mass. 1984).

6. However, see the criticism by William Nordhaus, "Can the Share Economy Conquer Stagflation?" *The Quarterly Journal of Economics* (February 1988).

7. This should be qualified. If industry A is a polluting and industry B is a nonpolluting industry, we should tax industry A at a higher rate than industry B to reflect the social costs imposed on society. Second, an ideal tax system would require differentiation on the basis of price elasticities of demand. The general rule would be that tax rates vary inversely with price elasticities of demand. However, this would be difficult to administer since it requires a firm knowledge of price elasticities by the tax authority. Furthermore, if we followed this rule, necessities would be taxed at higher rates than luxuries and could lead to increased inequality of incomes. This is politically unacceptable; witness the fact that current tax policy usually taxes luxuries at a higher rate than necessities.

8. "Americans and Japanese Save About the Same," *Wall Street Journal*, June 14, 1988, p. 30. The Federal Reserve, defining personal savings as the change in net worth, finds a much higher personal savings rate than the Department of Commerce, which defines personal savings as disposable income less personal consumption.

9. This same uncertainty holds for tax cuts on labor income. An increase in wages after taxes, resulting from a tax decrease, will have a "substitution effect" which will increase the supply of labor, that is, at

higher wages after taxes workers are willing to supply more labor. However, there is also an "income effect"—higher wage rates after taxes increase income—and workers will usually demand more leisure or less work. It is possible that the income effect will dominate the substitution effect so that less labor will be forthcoming at higher wages after taxes. Modern-day "supply-siders" put too much emphasis on the substitution effect.

10. See: Robert J. Barro, "Are Government Bonds Net Wealth?" *Journal of Political Economy* (November-December, 1974).

11. Lester Thurow, *The Zero-Sum Solution* (Simon and Schuster, New York, 1985), p. 277.

12. "Behold! We Have An Industrial Policy," *New York Times*, May 22, 1988, p. 29.

13. Henry Grabowski and John Vernon, "Longer Patents for Lower Imitation Barriers: The 1984 Drug Act," *American Economic Review* (May 1986).

9

Concluding Remarks

> I draw the conclusion that, assuming no important wars and no important increase in population, the *economic problem* may be solved, or be least within sight of solution, within a hundred years. This means that the economic problem is not—if we look into the future—*the permanent problem of the human race.*[1]

A quiet revolution is near at hand. It is expected that per capita GNP will increase by *at least* 2.5 percent annually over the next 25 or 30 years in the United States. Given the slow growth of the last 25 years or so, this forecast may appear "out of the ballpark." But if one comprehends the nature of the long Kondratieff cycle, this forecast is reasonable. Periods of about 25 to 30 years of slow growth alternate with periods of rapid growth. Examination of these long waves warrants the conclusion that in the early 1990s the United States and much of the world will experience the beginning of the rising phase of the fifth Kondratieff cycle.

The central and dominant force causing the higher per capita GNP growth rate will be the surging rate of technological advance. Technological advance will accelerate mainly because of the large and growing pool of basic research, widening the range of possible economic applications. In addition, the inevitable internationalization of the world economy will intensify competition among firms, compelling them to use the latest technology.

Other things being equal, the increasing rate of technological change will not only increase the rate of growth of per capita GNP, but will also lower interest rates and minimize the inflation and unemployment problems.

Some factors to be included in the portmanteau of "other things" are positive and will complement technological advance—thereby lending additional support to the forecast of higher per capita GNP growth rates. Changes in the age structure of the labor force will improve the quality of the labor force in the United States. Furthermore, the diminished level of discrimination against women and blacks will lead to significant improvements in labor productivity. We can also expect the improvement in educational achievement experienced in the last seven years in the United States to continue.

On the other hand, some factors included in "other things" may be negative, such as war, excess population growth, political turbulence, destabilizing economic policy, and depressions. War between the Soviet Union and the United States is unlikely. Examination of population data quickly dispels the belief in the existence of a "population bomb." Political turbulence will probably be muted by an economy that is operating in good order. Destabilizing economic policy, as in the early 1930s, can be repeated—though we must give politicians some credit for learning from the past. While we will no doubt experience recessions, these recessions will be more moderate than in the past because of the relative growth of the service sector. Prolonged depressions are highly unlikely.

More and more the world will look like a single integrated economy, with the multinational corporation being the major agent for changing economic and social relationships. There is no fundamental conflict between the pursuit of profits by multinational firms and economic welfare if markets are workably competitive. The high rates of growth in per capita GNP will not be confined to the United States, but will be largely a worldwide phenomenon. The reawakening of the Asian economies, the integration of the European economies, and the restructuring of the Soviet economy all dramatically illustrate the inevitable trend toward the integration of the world economy.

If the forecast that in the U.S. per capita GNP will increase by at least 2.5 percent materializes, the next generation of workers will have roughly twice the income of the current generation of workers. Many of the economic problems will diminish or perhaps even disappear. For example, with wage rates increasing faster than the price level, the social security system should be solvent—perhaps the system will even suffer from an embarrassment of its surplus. To take another example: Higher income levels will increase the tax base, so that the financing of public expenditures should be more manageable in the future compared with the present.

On average, over the next 25 or 30 years, we can expect labor markets to be tight. Real wages will rise at about the same rate of increase as the increase in technological advance (i.e., productivity). With technological advance accelerating, one would also expect the real wage rate to accelerate. For high school and college graduates equipped with a solid technical training and a broad liberal arts education, employment opportunities should be abundant. The liberal arts background often has many surprising applications on the job. In addition, the accelerating pace of technological advance will produce frequent changes in the demand for labor. The worker equipped with a liberal arts background will be more flexible and will find it easier to adjust to changing labor market requirements.

Financial markets should also probably be tight or bullish over the next two or three decades. The accelerating rate of technological advance will produce, on average, the expectation of declining interest rates. With a given level of profits, the expectation of lower interest rates is equivalent to the expectation that the price of stocks and bonds will increase.

If this forecast of high growth rates comes true, how will it affect human happiness or the sense of well-being? While individuals will no doubt have an increased sense of well-being, the increment in the sense of well-being will not rise at the same rate as real income. This is nothing more than the law of diminishing marginal utility, that is, increments of real income increase the sense of well-being, but at a diminishing rate. Furthermore, one's sense of well-being has a social dimension. If one's income increases more slowly than that of others, the sense of well-being may decrease. It is probably true that, after a certain income level is achieved, the sense of well-being is more closely related to the development of wholesome interpersonal relationships than to increments in income.

Diminished discrimination against women and blacks represents a sea change in human relationships. In the economy, questions of gender or skin color will become irrelevant and questions which relate to merit will become more important. And one would expect that, as women and blacks achieve equal opportunity, the quality of social relationships will improve.

The expected material prosperity of the next 25 or 30 years *can* be a powerful force in improving the quality of life. Whether it *will* be a powerful force is another question. Rapid economic development and prosperity will probably make the world safer for democracy. And we will have time for poetry and music and time to just "go fishin'." We will also have time to indulge in our worst instincts. The choices we make are basically uncertain. In spite of the uncertainty we should take a chance and "roll the dice." Prosperity makes civilization possible and perhaps even probable.

NOTE

1. J. M. Keynes, *Essays in Persuasion* (W. W. Norton, New York, 1963), pp. 365–66. (First published in 1931. Emphasis in the original.)

Bibliography

Arrow, Kenneth J. "The Theory of Discrimination." In *Discrimination in Labor Markets*, edited by Orley Ashenfelter and Arthur Rees. Princeton, N.J.: Princeton University Press, 1974.

Barro, Robert J. "Are Government Bonds Net Wealth?" *Journal of Political Economy*, November–December, 1974.

Batra, Ravi. *The Great Depression of 1990*. New York: Simon and Schuster, 1987.

Baumol, William J. "Macroeconomics of Unbalanced Growth: The Anatomy of the Urban Crisis," *American Economic Review* (June 1967).

———. "Productivity Growth, Convergence and Welfare: What the Long-Run Data Show," *American Economic Review* (December 1986).

Bertram, Gordon W. "Economic Growth in Canadian Industry, 1870–1915: The Staple Model and the Take-off Hypothesis," *Canadian Journal of Economics and Social Studies* (May 1963).

Bloom, Allan. *The Closing of the American Mind*. New York: Simon and Schuster, 1987.

Conrad, Alfred H. "Income Growth and Structural Change." In *American Economic History*, edited by Seymour E. Harris. New York: McGraw-Hill, 1961.

Dales, J. H. *Pollution, Property and Prices*. University of Toronto Press, 1968.

Darby, Michael. "The U.S. Productivity Slowdown," *American Economic Review* (June 1984).

Dewey, Edward and Edwin Dakin. *Cycles: The Science of Prediction*. New York: Henry Holt, 1947.

Dhrymes, Pheobus J. "A Comparison of Productivity Behavior in Manufacturing and Service Industries," *The Review of Economics and Statistics* (February 1963).

Domar, Evsey. *Essays in the Theory of Economic Growth.* New York: Oxford University Press, 1957.

Easterlin, R. A. "The Economics and Sociology of Fertility: A Synthesis," prepared for *Seminar in Early Industrialization,* Princeton University Press, 1972.

Enos, John. "Invention and Innovation in the Petroleum Refining Industry," in *The Rate and Direction of Inventive Activity.* Princeton, NJ: Princeton University Press, 1962.

Fair, Ray. "Sources of Economic Fluctuations in the United States," *Quarterly Journal of Economics* (May 1988).

Faulkner, Harold U. *American Economic History.* New York: Harper & Row, 1931.

Freeman, C. *The Role of Small Firms in Innovation in the United Kingdom Since 1945,* Research Report No. 6, HMSO, 1971.

Forrester, Jay. "How the Long-Wave Theory May Explain the Sluggishness of Capital Formation," *Financier* (September 1977).

Goldsmith, Raymond. *Historical and Comparative Rates of Production, Productivity and Prices,* 86th Congress, 1st Session, 1959, part 2.

Gordon, Robert J. *Macroeconomics,* 3rd ed. Boston: Little, Brown, 1984.

Grabowski, Henry and John Vernon. "Longer Patents for Lower Imitation Barriers: The 1984 Drug Act," *American Economic Review,* (May 1986).

Griliches, Zvi. "Research Costs and Social Returns: Hybrid Corn and Related Innovations," *Journal of Political Economy* (October 1958).

Hibbs, Douglas A. *The American Political Economy.* Cambridge, MA: Harvard University Press, 1987.

Historical Statistics of the United States, Colonial Times to 1970, Series F 1–5, U.S. Department of Commerce, 1971.

Hughes, Jonathon. *American Economic History.* 2nd ed. Glenview, IL: Scott, Foresman and Co., 1987.

Kahn, Herman. *World Economic Development.* Boulder, Colo: Westview Press, 1979.

Kaldor, N. and J. A. Mirrlees. "Growth Model with Induced Technical Progress," *Review of Economic Studies,* 29 (1961–62).

Kendrick, J. W. *Productivity Trends in the United States.* New York: Columbia University Press, 1973.

Kennedy, Paul. *The Rise and Fall of Great Powers.* New York: Random House, 1987.

Keynes, J. M. *Essays in Persuasion,* New York: W. W. Norton, 1963. (First published in 1931.)

———. *The General Theory of Employment, Interest and Money,* New York: Harcourt Brace, Jovanovich, 1936.

Klein, Lawrence R. and Joel Popkin. "An Econometric Analysis of the Postwar Relationship Between Inventory Fluctuations and Aggregate Economic Activity."In *Inventory Fluctuations and Economic Stabilization*. Joint Economic Committee, 87th Congress, 1st Session, 1961.

Klein, Lawrence R. *An Introduction to Econometrics*. Englewood Cliffs, NJ: Prentice-Hall, 1962.

Kondratieff, N. "The Long Waves in Economic Life," *Review of Economic Statistics* (November 1936).

Landau, Ralph. "Technology, Economics and Public Policy." In *Technology and Economic Policy*, edited by Ralph Landau and Dale W. Jorgenson. Cambridge, Mass.: Ballinger Publishing Co., 1986.

Lewis, W. A. "Economic Development with Unlimited Supplies of Labor," *Manchester School of Economics and Social Studies* (May 1954).

———. *Tropical Development 1880–1913: Studies in Economic Progress*. Winchester, Mass.: Allen and Unwin, 1978.

———. "The Slowing Down of the Engine of Growth," *American Economic Review* (March 1980).

Lynn, Frank. "An Investigation of the Rate of Development and Diffusion of Technology in Our Modern Industrial Society," *Report of the National Commission on Technology, Automation, and Economic Progress*, Washington, D.C., 1966.

Maddison, Angus. *Economic Growth in the West*. New York: W. W. Norton, 1964.

———. "Phases of Capitalistic Development," *Quarterly Review*, Banca Nazionale del Lavoro, no. 121 (June 1977).

Mansfield, Edwin. *The Economics of Technological Change*. New York: W. W. Norton, 1968.

Meadows, Donella H., Dennis L. Meadows, Jorgen Randers, and William W. Behrens III, *The Limits of Growth*. New York: New American Library, 1972.

Metzler, Lloyd A. "The Nature and Stability of Inventory Cycles," *Review of Economics and Statistics*, 23 (June 1941).

Mikesell, Raymond F. and James E. Zinser. "The Nature of the Savings Function in Developing Countries: A Survey of the Theoretical and Empirical Literature," *The Journal of Economic Literature* (March 1973).

Munnell, Alicia. "The Outlook for Social Security in the Wake of the 1983 Amendments." In *The Economics of Aging*, edited by Myron H. Ross. The W. E. Upjohn Institute for Employment Research, 1985.

Nordhaus, William. "Can the Share Economy Conquer Stagflation?" *The Quarterly Journal of Economics* (February 1988).

Nordhaus, William and James Tobin. *Is Growth Obsolete?* National Bureau of Economic Research, 1972.

North, Douglas C. *The Economic Growth of the United States, 1970– 1861.* New York: W. W. Norton, 1966.

Olson, Mancur. *The Rise and Decline of Nations.* New Haven, CT: Yale University Press, 1982.

Phelps, E. S. "The Statistical Theory of Racism and Sexism," *American Economic Review* (September 1972).

Press, Frank, "Technological Competition and the Western Alliance." In *A High Technology Gap? Europe, America, Japan,* edited by Andrew J. Pierre. New York: New York University Press, 1987.

Reich, Robert, "Behold! We Have an Industrial Policy," *New York Times,* May 22, 1988.

Reynolds, Lloyd G. "The Spread of Economic Growth in the Third World: 1850–1980," *Journal of Economic Literature* (September 1983).

Robertson, D. H. *Banking Policy and the Price Level.* New York: Augustus M. Kelley, 1949.

Scherer, F. M. *Innovation and Growth.* Cambridge, Mass. MIT Press, 1984.

Schlesinger, Arthur M. *The Cycles of American History.* Boston: Houghton Mifflin, 1986.

Schlesinger, James R. and Almarin Phillips. "The Ebb Tide of Capitalism? Schumpeter's Prophecy Re-examined," *Quarterly Journal of Economics* (August 1959).

Schumpeter, Joseph. "The Analysis of Economic Change," *The Review of Economic Statistics* (1935). Reprinted in *Readings in Business Cycle Theory.* Philadelphia: The Blakiston Co., 1944.

———. *Business Cycles.* New York: McGraw-Hill, 1939.

———. *Capitalism, Socialism and Democracy.* New York: Harper & Row, 1947.

Simon, Julian. *The Ultimate Resource.* Princeton, N.J.: Princeton University Press, 1981.

Singer, Max. "Don't Be Misled by Africa," *Wall Street Journal,* January 28, 1988.

Smith, Adam. *The Wealth of Nations.* New York: Modern Library, 1964.

Smith, James P. "Race and Human Capital," *American Economic Review* (September 1984).

Soete, L. L.G. "Firm Size and Inventive Activity: the Evidence Reconsidered," *European Economic Review* 12 (1961).

Stigler, G. J. and G. S. Becker, "De Gustibus Non Est Disputandum," *American Economic Review* (March 1977).

Thurow, Lester C. *The Zero-Sum Solution.* New York: Simon and Schuster, 1985.

Toffler, Alvin. *Future Shock.* New York: Bantam Books, 1970.

Toynbee, Arnold. *A Study of History.* New York: Oxford University Press, 1947.

Vasko, Tibor. (ed.) *The Long-Wave Debate*. New York: Springer-Verlag, 1987.

Viner, Jacob. *The Long View and the Short*. New York: Free Press, 1958.

Wattenberg, B. *The Birth Dearth*. New York: Pharos Books, 1987.

Weitzman, Martin. *The Share Economy*. Cambridge, Mass.: Harvard University Press, 1984.

Wiener, Norbert. *The Human Use of Human Beings*. Boston: Houghton Mifflin, 1950.

Young, Robert B. "Product Growth Cycles—A Key to Growth Planning," Stanford Research Institute, undated. Cited by Alvin Toffler, *Future Shock*. New York: Bantam Books, 1970.

Index

ABOUT THE AUTHOR

MYRON H. ROSS is professor of economics at Western Michigan University in Kalamazoo. He has had extensive experience as an economic consultant and for the past two decades has served as a land commissioner in the federal courts. In 1967–68 he was a visiting Fulbright scholar in Yugoslavia.

Professor Ross has written widely in the areas of theoretical and applied economics, and his articles have appeared in the *American Economic Review*, the *Journal of Political Economy*, the *Quarterly Journal of Economics*, and *Economic Inquiry*, among others. He is the author of a text in macroeconomics, *Income: Analysis and Policy*. Professor Ross holds a B.A. and M.A. from Temple University and a Ph.D. from the University of Pennsylvania.